Cake!

_____

Also in This Series

Family Favorite Casserole Recipes:
103 Comforting Breakfast Casseroles, Dinner Ideas,
and Desserts Everyone Will Love

No-Bake Desserts:
103 Easy Recipes for No-Bake Cookies, Bars, and Treats

Everyday Dinner Ideas:
103 Easy Recipes for Chicken, Pasta, and Other Dishes Everyone Will Love

Easy Cookie Recipes:
103 Best Recipes for Chocolate Chip Cookies, Cake Mix Creations,
Bars, and Holiday Treats Everyone Will Love

Retro Recipes from the '50s and '60s:
103 Vintage Appetizers, Dinners, and Drinks Everyone Will Love

Essential Slow Cooker Recipes:
103 Fuss-Free Slow Cooker Meals Everyone Will Love

Easy Chicken Recipes:
103 Inventive Soups, Salads, Casseroles, and Dinners Everyone Will Love

Homemade Soup Recipes:
103 Easy Recipes for Soups, Stews, Chilis, and Chowders Everyone Will Love

The Lighten Up Cookbook:
103 Easy, Slimmed-Down Favorites for Breakfast, Lunch, and
Dinner Everyone Will Love

Festive Holiday Recipes:
103 Must-Make Dishes for Thanksgiving, Christmas, and
New Year's Eve Everyone Will Love

Cake!

103 Decadent Recipes for
Poke Cakes, Dump Cakes, Everyday Cakes,
and Special Occasion Cakes
Everyone Will Love

Addie Gundry

St. Martin's Griffin ☙ New York

CAKE! Copyright © 2018 by Prime Publishing, LLC.
All rights reserved. Printed in the United States of America. For information,
address St. Martin's Press, 175 Fifth Avenue, New York, N.Y. 10010.

www.stmartins.com

Photography by Megan Von Schönhoff and Tom Krawczyk

The Library of Congress Cataloging-in-Publication Data is available upon request.

ISBN 978-1-250-16196-3 (trade paperback)
ISBN 978-1-250-16197-0 (ebook)

Our books may be purchased in bulk for promotional, educational, or business
use. Please contact your local bookseller or the Macmillan Corporate and
Premium Sales Department at 1-800-221-7945, extension 5442, or by email at
MacmillanSpecialMarkets@macmillan.com.

First Edition: October 2018

10 9 8 7 6 5 4 3 2 1

To Megan, photographer extraordinaire.
Thank you for your talent.
Your vision and skill are as beautiful
as the photos you take.

Contents

Introduction   1

1
Coffee Cakes

Sour Cream Coffee Cake   4

Cinnamon Apple Crumb Cake   7

Cherry Coffee Cake   8

Buttermilk Blueberry Coffee Cake   11

Cranberry-Pecan Coffee Cake   12

Pecan Pie Coffee Cake   15

2
Bundt Cakes and Pound Cakes

Kentucky Butter Cake   18

Lime Bundt Cake   21

Samoa Bundt Cake   22

Peach Pound Cake   25

Cream Cheese Red Velvet Cake   26

Neapolitan Bundt Cake   29

Pink Lemonade Bundt Cakes   30

Classic Buttery Pound Cake   33

Cinnamon Roll Pound Cake   34

Brownie Butter Cake   37

Italian Lemon Mini Pound Cakes   38

Coconut Pound Cake   41

Southern Pecan Pound Cake   42

Chocolate Pound Cake   45

Cherry 7UP Pound Cake   46

3
Old-Fashioned Cakes

Grandma's Famous Jimmy Cake   50

1970s Harvey Wallbanger Cake   53

Lemon Crazy Cake   54

Grandmother's Lazy Daisy Cake   57

Dandy Diner Dream Cake   58

Pineapple Upside-Down Cake   61

The Best Angel Food Cake   62

Creamy Lemon Angel Cake   65

Victoria Sponge Cake   66

Old-Fashioned Fruitcake   69

Refrigerator Fudge Cake   70

Lemon Shortcake Icebox Cake   73

No-Bake Strawberry Icebox Cake   74

Pistachio Icebox Cake   77

4
Everyday Cakes

Classic Texas Sheet Cake   80

Amish Applesauce Cake   83

Grandma's Magic Cake   84

Lemon Poppy Seed Cake   87

Church Cake   88

Best-Ever German Chocolate Cake   91

Texas Tornado Cake   92

Inside-Out Cream Puff Cake   95

Cinnamon Roll Cake Roll   96

Almond Honey Cake   99

Zucchini Cake with Browned Butter Frosting   100

Millionaire Marshmallow Fluff Cake   103

Moist, Fluffy Coconut Cake   104

Blueberry Angel Food Sheet Cake   107

Heaven and Hell Cake   108

Italian Love Cake   111

Mint Patty Cake   112

Cinnamon Cream Cheese Apple Cake   115

Glazed Rum Cake   116

Classic Chocolate Cake   119

No-Bake Chocolate Éclair Cake   120

5
Dump Cakes, Poke Cakes, and Mug Cakes

Apple Pie Dump Cake with Pecan Topping   124

Hubby's Favorite Dump Cake   127

Funfetti Dump Cake   128

Piña Colada Dump Cake   131

Snickers Poke Cake   132

Fall Pumpkin Dump Cake   135

Slow Cooker Chocolate Lava Cake   136

Slow Cooker Vanilla-Caramel Poke Cake   139

Chocolate Turtle Poke Cake   140

Oreo Pudding Poke Cake   143

Strawberry Jell-O Poke Cake   144

Banana Pudding Poke Cake   147

Cannoli Poke Cake   148

Carrot Cake Poke Cake   151

Snickerdoodle Mug Cake   152

Four-Ingredient Molten Nutella Lava Cake   155

Moist Vanilla Mug Cake   156

Cookies 'n' Cream Mug Cake   159

Fudgy S'mores Mug Cake   160

The Best Pumpkin Mug Cake   163

6
Special Occasion Cakes

Lemon Chiffon Layer Cake   166

Dreamsicle Cake   169

Southern Caramel Cake   170

Strawberry–Chocolate Mousse Cake   173

Black Forest Cake   174

Gooiest Butter Cake   177

Chocolate Oreo Cake   178

Peanut Butter Cup Cake   181

Pumpkin Angel Food Cake   182

Key Lime Angel Food Cake   185

Hot Chocolate Cake   186

Oreo Icebox Dessert   189

Peanut Butter Lover's Icebox Cake   190

Boston Cream Pie   193

Homemade Strawberry Shortcakes   194

Buttermilk Spice Layer Cake   197

Ultimate Cookie Layer Cake   198

Birthday Funfetti Layer Cake   201

Loaded Chocolate Chip Cookie Cake   202

Baby Shower Cake   205

Bouquet of Roses Cake   206

Rice Krispies Cake   209

Carrot Cake Roll   210

Mardi Gras King Cake   213

Firecracker Cake   214

Gingerbread Cake   217

Christmas Vanilla Cake Roll   218

Acknowledgments   220

Index   221

About the Author   226

Cake!

Introduction

Julia Child once said, "A party without a cake is just a meeting," and I couldn't agree more. Not only is cake one of my favorite foods, it is also one of the prettiest, and just the sight of a cake shouts "celebration." With endless opportunities to make a cake something special, I have spent a lot of my personal and professional life making and eating cakes.

I don't remember, but I am sure there is a picture of me somewhere eating my first piece of cake at my first birthday party. I do have memories of pure sugar birthday bliss as I got a little older, and to this day my favorite kind of cake is vanilla with vanilla frosting—preferably the inexpensive kind at the grocery store that is so sweet it'll rot your teeth just as it's bringing a big smile to your face. Although it's tough to beat the sweet simplicity of a white cake, I have spent many years making a variety of unique and exciting cakes. Last year I made a Birthday Funfetti Layer Cake (page 201) for my birthday. Over the holidays I always make a Buttermilk Spice Layer Cake (page 197) and the Fourth of July is not the same without Firecracker Cake (page 214). Some cakes, like Dandy Diner Dream Cake (page 58) take a bit of effort, while others, like Apple Pie Dump Cake with Pecan Topping (page 124) are simple enough to throw together in about 10 minutes. Whether you're ready to settle in for a relaxing day in the kitchen or you're just looking for the quickest way to get a sweet treat, you're sure to find a cake in this book for any mood.

A cake, when given to a friend or served to family, is a symbol of festivity and love. Cakes find their way into the most important milestones in people's lives, from anniversaries to graduations to weddings. They have a home in any and every entertaining occasion as well—not just those special occasions, but the casual ones too. It's those impromptu gatherings, the chaotic events, the outdoor picnics, the inside dinners, and the late-night gatherings, where cakes truly find their place to shine.

Why does this book feature 103 cake recipes? When you come to my house for dinner, I want you to know you can always bring a friend, or two, or three . . . and for those who have been to my home, you know firsthand that guests tend to multiply as the food continues to come out of the oven and cocktails are poured. One hundred recipes felt too rigid, too finite. By adding the extra three it became more welcoming, a reminder that there is always more room at the table, and there should always be a cake at the center of it.

—Addie

1

Coffee Cakes

I have such a fondness for coffee cakes, probably because I associate them with special occasions, whether it's Christmas morning and everyone's still in their jammies or it's a quiet Sunday where I get to sleep in before getting started with my day. They add some pep in my step in the mornings, so it's always a joy to prepare my favorites.

Sour Cream Coffee Cake

Yield: Serves 8 | Prep Time: 20 minutes | Cook Time: 40 minutes

Sour cream adds density and moisture to a cake, which works well to differentiate a coffee cake from a fluffy dessert cake. The streusel topping adds a sweet cinnamon crunch to start off the morning.

INGREDIENTS

Cake

8 tablespoons (1 stick) unsalted butter, softened

¾ cup granulated sugar

2 large eggs

1 teaspoon vanilla bean paste or vanilla extract

½ cup sour cream

1¼ cups all-purpose flour

1 teaspoon baking powder

¼ teaspoon baking soda

¼ teaspoon kosher salt

Streusel

½ cup raisins (optional)

½ cup chopped walnuts

½ cup all-purpose flour

¼ cup packed light brown sugar

3 tablespoons unsalted butter, cut in cubes, cold

1½ teaspoons ground cinnamon

¼ teaspoon ground nutmeg

¼ teaspoon kosher salt

Glaze

½ cup confectioners' sugar

3–4 tablespoons maple syrup

DIRECTIONS

1. Preheat the oven to 350°F. Grease a 9 × 5-inch loaf pan. Line the pan with parchment paper, leaving an overhang on the long sides.

2. *For the cake:* Using a hand mixer or a stand mixer fitted with the paddle attachment, cream the butter with the sugar until fluffy. Add the eggs, one at a time, until mixed in. Add the vanilla and sour cream and mix well.

3. In a medium bowl, whisk together the flour, baking powder, baking soda, and salt. Add the flour mixture to the butter mixture and beat until combined; do not overmix.

4. *For the streusel topping:* In another medium bowl, combine the raisins, if using, walnuts, flour, brown sugar, butter, cinnamon, nutmeg, and salt. Using a pastry cutter or fork, mix until crumbly.

5. Pour half of the batter into the loaf pan and then top with half of the streusel topping. Add the remaining batter, then sprinkle with the rest of the streusel topping.

6. Bake for 40 minutes or until a toothpick inserted in the center comes out clean. Let the cake cool in the pan for 10 to 15 minutes. Using the parchment as a handle, transfer the cake to a wire rack and let it cool completely. Transfer to a serving plate.

7. *For the glaze:* In a small bowl, mix the confectioners' sugar with 3 tablespoons of the maple syrup, adding more syrup as needed for a pourable consistency. Drizzle over the cooled cake. Slice and serve.

Cinnamon Apple Crumb Cake

Yield: Serves 8 | Prep Time: 20 minutes | Cook Time: 35 to 40 minutes

The chunks of apple in this cake remind me of the texture of apple pie: soft, warm, and full of cinnamon-y goodness. The brown butter glaze on top seals in all of the sweet flavors.

INGREDIENTS

Cinnamon Streusel Crumb

1½ cups all-purpose flour

½ cup chopped walnuts

½ cup packed dark brown sugar

¼ cup granulated sugar

1 teaspoon ground cinnamon

½ teaspoon kosher salt

¼ teaspoon ground cardamom

¼ teaspoon ground nutmeg

8 tablespoons (1 stick) unsalted butter, melted

½ teaspoon vanilla bean paste or vanilla extract

Cake

4 tablespoons unsalted butter, softened

½ cup sugar

1 large egg

½ cup sour cream

1 teaspoon vanilla bean paste or vanilla extract

1 cup all-purpose flour

½ teaspoon baking powder

¼ teaspoon baking soda

¼ teaspoon salt

1 large apple, peeled, cored, and chopped

Brown Butter Glaze

3 tablespoons unsalted butter

1 cup confectioners' sugar

2 teaspoons vanilla bean paste or vanilla extract

2 tablespoons heavy cream

DIRECTIONS

1. Preheat the oven to 350°F. Grease an 8-inch springform pan. Line the pan with parchment paper and lightly grease.

2. *For the cinnamon streusel crumb:* Mix the flour, walnuts, brown sugar, sugar, cinnamon, salt, cardamom, and nutmeg in a medium bowl. Add the melted butter and vanilla and toss.

3. *For the cake:* Using a hand mixer or a stand mixer fitted with the paddle attachment, beat the butter with the sugar on medium speed until fluffy. Add the egg and mix well. Add the sour cream and vanilla and mix well. In a medium bowl, whisk together the flour, baking powder, baking soda, and salt. Reduce the speed to low. Add the flour mixture to the butter mixture and beat until combined.

4. Spread half of the batter in the bottom of the pan. Sprinkle the chopped apple over the batter. Sprinkle 1 cup of the cinnamon streusel over the apple. Spread the remaining batter over the crumbs, then add the rest of the cinnamon streusel.

5. Bake for 35 to 40 minutes or until a toothpick inserted in the center of the cake comes out clean. Let the cake cool in the pan for 10 to 15 minutes, then remove the ring from the sides and let it cool completely. Transfer to a serving plate.

6. *For the brown butter glaze:* Heat the butter in a small saucepan, stirring continuously, until the butter begins to brown, being careful not to let it burn. Transfer to a small bowl. Whisk in the confectioners' sugar and vanilla, then the cream. Drizzle over the crumb cake. Slice and serve.

Cherry Coffee Cake

Yield: Serves 12 | Prep Time: 15 minutes | Cook Time: 35 to 45 minutes

While I used cherry pie filling for this particular recipe, it's a versatile dish, so you can make it any flavor you'd like. Exchange cherry pie filling for blueberry pie filling or apple pie filling with a hint of cinnamon. Make this coffee cake your own!

INGREDIENTS

2 cups all-purpose flour

½ cup plus 2 tablespoons sugar

2 teaspoons baking powder

½ teaspoon kosher salt

8 tablespoons (1 stick) unsalted butter, melted

¼ cup finely chopped almonds

2 large eggs, beaten

½ cup milk

¼ teaspoon almond extract

1 (21-ounce) can cherry pie filling

DIRECTIONS

1. Preheat the oven to 325°F. Lightly grease a 9 × 13-inch baking dish.

2. In a medium bowl, whisk together the flour, sugar, baking powder, and salt. Add the melted butter and stir until the mixture is crumbly. Transfer ½ cup of the dry mixture to a small bowl, add the almonds, and stir to combine. Set aside.

3. In a small bowl, whisk the eggs, milk, and almond extract together. Add to the flour mixture and stir to combine. Pour the batter into the baking dish. Spread the cherry pie filling over the top. Sprinkle the reserved almond mixture over the pie filling.

4. Bake for 35 to 45 minutes or until the top is golden and the cake is set. Let cool on a wire rack for 5 to 10 minutes. Slice and serve.

Buttermilk Blueberry Coffee Cake

Yield: Serves 9 | Prep Time: 15 minutes | Cook Time: 35 to 40 minutes

Buttermilk gives this coffee cake a soft texture with lots of body, which makes this a buoyant, airy option for breakfast. I use fresh blueberries in this recipe, but you could easily switch those out for raspberries or blackberries.

INGREDIENTS

8 tablespoons (1 stick) unsalted butter, softened

¾ cup plus 3 tablespoons sugar

1 tablespoon grated lemon zest

1 large egg

½ teaspoon vanilla bean paste or vanilla extract

½ teaspoon almond extract

2 cups fresh blueberries

2 cups all-purpose flour

2 teaspoons baking powder

1 teaspoon kosher salt

½ cup buttermilk

DIRECTIONS

1. Preheat the oven to 350°F. Lightly grease a 9-inch square baking dish.

2. Using a hand mixer or a stand mixer fitted with the paddle attachment, beat the butter with ¾ cup plus 2 tablespoons of the sugar and the lemon zest on medium speed until fluffy. Beat in the egg, vanilla, and almond extract.

3. In a small bowl, toss the blueberries with ¼ cup of the flour. In a separate bowl, whisk the remaining 1¾ cups flour with the baking powder and salt. On low speed, add the flour mixture to the butter mixture in 3 batches, alternating with the buttermilk in 2 batches, beating until combined. Fold in the blueberries. Spread the batter into the baking dish. Sprinkle the remaining 1 tablespoon sugar over the batter.

4. Bake for 35 to 40 minutes or until the cake is golden and a toothpick inserted in the center comes out clean. Let the cake cool for 5 minutes. Slice and serve.

Cranberry-Pecan Coffee Cake

Yield: Serves 16 | Prep Time: 20 minutes | Cook Time: 50 minutes to 1 hour

The tart combination of cranberries with a bit of orange zest acts as a welcome wake-up call in the morning. And the sugar glaze makes this sweet enough to have a slice for dessert.

INGREDIENTS

Streusel

6 tablespoons unsalted butter, softened

1 cup packed light brown sugar

1½ teaspoons ground cinnamon

½ teaspoon ground nutmeg

½ teaspoon minced crystallized ginger

1 cup chopped pecans

Cake

2 cups all-purpose flour, plus extra for the pan

8 tablespoons (1 stick) unsalted butter, softened

¾ cup granulated sugar

1 teaspoon vanilla bean paste or vanilla extract

3 large eggs

1 teaspoon baking powder

1 teaspoon baking soda

1 cup sour cream

2 teaspoons grated orange zest

1 cup fresh or thawed frozen cranberries

DIRECTIONS

1. Preheat the oven to 350°F. Grease and flour a 6-cup tube pan.

2. *For the streusel:* In a small bowl, stir together the butter, brown sugar, cinnamon, nutmeg, ginger, and pecans. Set aside.

3. *For the cake:* Using a hand mixer or a stand mixer fitted with the paddle attachment, cream the butter on medium speed for 1 to 2 minutes. Add the sugar and vanilla and beat until light and fluffy. Add the eggs one at a time and beat until combined.

4. In a large bowl, whisk together the flour, baking powder, and baking soda. On low speed, add the flour mixture to the butter mixture in 3 batches, alternating with the sour cream in 2 batches, beating until combined. Add the orange zest and beat to incorporate.

5. Spread half of the batter in the tube pan. Sprinkle half of the cranberries then half the streusel over the batter. Cover with the remaining batter, streusel, and cranberries.

6. Bake for 50 minutes to 1 hour or until the cake is golden and a toothpick inserted in the center comes out clean.

7. Let the cake cool completely in the pan on a wire rack, then transfer to a serving plate. Slice and serve.

Pecan Pie Coffee Cake

Yield: Serves 10 to 12 | Prep Time: 30 minutes | Cook Time: 40 to 45 minutes

The best part of a pecan pie is the addicting combination of crunchy and smooth that makes the texture so compelling. That same profile shines in this recipe, with a hard pecan topping contrasted against the smooth buttermilk cake.

INGREDIENTS

Cake

1¼ cups all-purpose flour

½ teaspoon baking powder

¼ teaspoon baking soda

¼ teaspoon kosher salt

¾ cup granulated sugar

2 ounces cream cheese, room temperature

3 tablespoons unsalted butter, softened

1 large egg plus 1 large egg white

1 teaspoon vanilla bean paste or vanilla extract

½ cup buttermilk

¼ cup sour cream

Topping

⅓ cup light corn syrup

¼ cup packed dark brown sugar

2 tablespoons unsalted butter

½ teaspoon ground cinnamon

1 cup coarsely chopped pecans

1 large egg, beaten

Pinch kosher salt

Confectioners' sugar for dusting

DIRECTIONS

1. Preheat the oven to 350°F. Grease a 9-inch round cake pan.

2. *For the cake:* In a small bowl, whisk together the flour, baking powder, baking soda, and salt. Using a hand mixer or a stand mixer fitted with the paddle attachment, beat the sugar, cream cheese, and butter on medium-low speed until light. Add the egg and white and beat well. Blend in the vanilla. In a liquid measuring cup, whisk together the buttermilk and sour cream.

3. On low speed, add the flour mixture to the cream cheese mixture in 3 batches, alternating with the buttermilk mixture in 2 batches; beat until blended (do not overmix).

4. Pour the batter into the cake pan and bake for 30 to 35 minutes or until the cake is golden and a toothpick inserted in the center comes out clean. Transfer the cake to a wire rack. Lower the oven temperature to 325°F.

5. *For the topping:* In a large microwave-safe bowl, combine the corn syrup, brown sugar, butter, and cinnamon. Microwave for 1 minute. Stir until the mixture is smooth. Stir in ½ cup of the pecans, egg, and salt. Using a wooden skewer, poke several holes in the cake. Pour the topping over the cake. Sprinkle the remaining ½ cup pecans on top. Bake for 10 minutes.

6. Let the cake cool completely in the pan. Dust with confectioners' sugar. Slice and serve.

2

Bundt Cakes and Pound Cakes

Bundt cakes are the ultimate party cakes. Their unique shape
allows the cake to stand out whenever it's put on display, and there
are always plenty of pieces to go around. Plus, you can stash little
treats or candies in the center for a pretty presentation!

And while some may call pound cakes old-fashioned,
I like to think of them as stylishly retro. Their sweet flavor and
dense texture make them a treat you can enjoy as is, or you
can dress them up with frosting and glaze if you wish.

Kentucky Butter Cake

Yield: Serves 12　│　Prep Time: 15 minutes　│　Cook Time: 1 hour 5 minutes to 1¼ hours

The butter in this recipe gives the cake extra moisture, so it's as soft and perfect as can be. Eating this cake is like eating a pound cake or an oversized doughnut.

INGREDIENTS

Cake

3 cups all-purpose flour, plus extra for the pan

2 cups granulated sugar

16 tablespoons (2 sticks) unsalted butter, softened

1 cup buttermilk

4 large eggs

1 tablespoon vanilla bean paste or vanilla extract

1 teaspoon kosher salt

1 teaspoon baking powder

½ teaspoon baking soda

Glaze

¾ cup granulated sugar

5 tablespoons plus 1 teaspoon unsalted butter

2 teaspoons vanilla bean paste or vanilla extract

Confectioners' sugar for dusting

Caramel sauce, warm, for drizzling

DIRECTIONS

1. Preheat the oven to 325°F. Grease and flour a 12-cup Bundt pan.

2. *For the cake:* Using a hand mixer or a stand mixer fitted with the paddle attachment, beat the flour, sugar, butter, buttermilk, eggs, vanilla, salt, baking powder, and baking soda on low speed for 1 minute. Increase the speed to medium and mix until smooth.

3. Pour the batter into the Bundt pan and bake for 1 hour 5 minutes to 1¼ hours or until the cake is golden and a toothpick inserted in the center comes out clean.

4. *For the glaze:* When the cake is done baking, place the granulated sugar, butter, vanilla, and 2 tablespoons water in a small saucepan. Heat over medium-low heat until the butter is melted and the sugar is dissolved.

5. While the cake is still warm, poke several holes in the cake with a wooden skewer, then pour the butter glaze over the cake.

6. Let the cake cool completely in the pan. Invert the cooled cake onto a serving plate. Dust with confectioners' sugar and drizzle with caramel sauce. Slice and serve.

Lime Bundt Cake

Yield: Serves 8 to 10 | Prep Time: 20 minutes | Cook Time: 40 to 45 minutes

This unique cake is a hit at parties. I've made it for different spring holidays like Saint Patrick's Day and Easter, and it's also fitting for celebrating Halloween or Christmas. The lime zest provides a cheerful burst of flavor that works well for entertaining, too.

INGREDIENTS

Cake

All-purpose flour for the pan

1 (15.25-ounce) box white or French vanilla cake mix

1 cup lime yogurt or sour cream

½ cup vegetable or canola oil

4 large eggs

1 tablespoon grated lime zest plus 1 tablespoon lime juice

Glaze

2 cups confectioners' sugar

4 ounces cream cheese, room temperature

4 tablespoons unsalted butter, softened

2 tablespoons grated lime zest plus ¼ cup lime juice

DIRECTIONS

1. Preheat the oven to 350°F. Grease and flour a 12-cup Bundt pan.

2. *For the cake:* Using a hand mixer or a stand mixer fitted with the paddle attachment, beat the cake mix, yogurt, oil, eggs, and lime zest and juice on low speed for 1 minute. Increase speed to medium and beat for 2 minutes. Pour the batter into the Bundt pan.

3. Bake for 40 to 45 minutes or until the cake is golden and a toothpick inserted in the center comes out clean. Let the cake cool in the pan for 15 minutes. Invert onto a wire rack and let cool completely.

4. *For the glaze:* In a large bowl, beat the confectioners' sugar, cream cheese, butter, and lime zest and juice until it's smooth and pourable, but thick.

5. Transfer the cake to a serving plate and drizzle the glaze over the cake. Slice and serve.

Samoa Bundt Cake

Yield: Serves 16 | Prep Time: 30 minutes | Cook Time: 50 minutes to 1 hour

I've learned to never bring Girl Scout cookies home because I can never bring home enough. During the fall after all of the cookies have disappeared, I like to make my husband this cake to help tide him over until the next year.

INGREDIENTS

Cake

2 cups all-purpose flour, plus extra for the pan

1 cup semisweet chocolate chips

½ cup bittersweet chocolate chips

8 tablespoons (1 stick) unsalted butter, softened

2 cups packed light brown sugar

3 large eggs

1 teaspoon baking soda

½ teaspoon kosher salt

1 cup sour cream

1 cup hot water

1 teaspoon espresso powder

1 teaspoon vanilla bean paste or vanilla extract

Frosting

12 tablespoons (1½ sticks) unsalted butter, softened

¼ cup caramel sauce, plus extra for drizzling

3 cups confectioners' sugar

1½–2 tablespoons heavy cream

1½ cups shredded coconut, toasted

Hot fudge sauce for drizzling

DIRECTIONS

1. Preheat the oven to 350°F. Grease and flour a 6-cup Bundt pan.

2. *For the cake:* Combine the chocolate chips in a microwave-safe bowl and heat in 20-second intervals until melted.

3. Using a hand mixer or a stand mixer fitted with the paddle attachment, beat the butter on medium speed for 1 minute. Add the brown sugar and beat until fluffy, about 5 minutes. Beat the eggs in one at a time. Beat in the melted chocolate until combined.

4. In a small bowl, whisk the flour, baking soda, and salt. On low speed, add the flour mixture to the butter mixture in 3 batches, alternating with the sour cream in 2 batches; beat until blended. Slowly add the hot water, espresso powder, and vanilla and beat to combine. Pour the batter into the Bundt pan.

5. Bake for 50 minutes to 1 hour or until a toothpick inserted in the center comes out clean. Let the cake cool in the pan for 10 minutes. Invert the cake onto a wire rack and let cool completely.

6. *For the frosting:* Using a hand mixer or a stand mixer fitted with the paddle attachment, beat the butter and caramel sauce on medium speed until smooth and creamy. Slowly beat in the confectioners' sugar, then add enough cream to create a spreadable consistency.

7. Place the cake on a serving plate. Spread the frosting on the cake and sprinkle the toasted coconut over the entire cake. Drizzle with caramel and hot fudge sauce. Slice and serve.

NOTES

You may need to heat the caramel and hot fudge sauces so they're the right consistency to drizzle over the cake.

To toast the coconut, spread it on a baking sheet and bake at 350°F for 5 to 10 minutes or until light golden brown.

Peach Pound Cake

Yield: Serves 12 | Prep Time: 20 minutes | Cook Time: 1 hour 20 minutes to 1 hour 40 minutes

While this may look like a cake on the outside, I like to see it as a giant version of biscotti. The pound cake–style gives the cake more density, similar to how biscotti has a denser consistency than a regular cookie, while the vanilla and almond extracts add a warm, sweet flavor.

INGREDIENTS

Cake

3 cups all-purpose flour, plus extra for the pan

2 cups peeled, diced peaches, fresh or thawed frozen

¼ cup packed light brown sugar

1 teaspoon ground cinnamon

24 tablespoons (3 sticks) unsalted butter, softened

3 cups granulated sugar

6 large eggs, room temperature

½ teaspoon kosher salt

¼ teaspoon baking soda

1 cup sour cream

1 teaspoon vanilla bean paste or vanilla extract

1 teaspoon almond extract

Glaze

1½ cups confectioners' sugar

1–3 tablespoons heavy cream

DIRECTIONS

1. Preheat the oven to 325°F. Grease and flour a 12-cup Bundt pan.

2. *For the cake:* In a small bowl, mix the peaches with the brown sugar and cinnamon; set aside. Using a hand mixer or a stand mixer fitted with the paddle attachment, beat the butter on medium speed until creamy. Add the sugar and beat until fluffy, about 7 minutes. Beat the eggs in one at a time.

3. In a medium bowl, whisk together the flour, salt, and baking soda. On low speed, add the flour mixture to the butter mixture in 3 batches, alternating with the sour cream in 2 batches, beating until combined. Beat in the vanilla, almond extract, and the peaches. Using a large spatula, give the batter a final stir to fully incorporate the peaches. Pour the batter into the Bundt pan.

4. Bake for 1 hour 20 minutes to 1 hour 40 minutes or until the cake is golden and a toothpick inserted in the center comes out clean. Let cool in the pan for 10 to 15 minutes. Invert onto a wire rack and let cool completely. Transfer to a serving plate.

5. *For the glaze:* In a small bowl, whisk the confectioners' sugar with enough cream to create a pourable consistency. Drizzle the glaze over the cooled cake. Slice and serve.

Cream Cheese Red Velvet Cake

Yield: Serves 10 to 12 | Prep Time: 20 minutes | Cook Time: 45 to 55 minutes

Red velvet cake is a showstopper all on its own, but what your friends and family aren't expecting is the cream cheese surprise in the center. The glaze on top seals it all in.

INGREDIENTS

Cream Cheese Filling

1 (8-ounce) package cream cheese, room temperature

⅓ cup granulated sugar

1 large egg

2 tablespoons all-purpose flour

½ teaspoon vanilla bean paste or vanilla extract

Cake

2½ cups all-purpose flour, plus extra for the pan

1¾ cups granulated sugar

2 tablespoons cocoa powder

1 teaspoon baking soda

1 teaspoon kosher salt

1 cup buttermilk

1 cup vegetable oil

2 large eggs

1 teaspoon white vinegar

1 teaspoon vanilla bean paste or vanilla extract

1½ tablespoons red liquid food coloring

Cream Cheese Glaze

4 ounces cream cheese, room temperature

½ cup confectioners' sugar

½ cup sour cream

1 teaspoon vanilla bean paste or vanilla extract

DIRECTIONS

1. Preheat the oven to 350°F. Grease and flour a 12-cup Bundt pan. Set aside.

2. *For the cream cheese filling:* Using a hand mixer or a stand mixer fitted with the paddle attachment, beat the cream cheese on medium speed for 1 to 2 minutes. Add the sugar and beat until fluffy. Add the egg, flour, and vanilla and beat until smooth. Set aside.

3. *For the cake:* In a large bowl, whisk together the flour, sugar, cocoa, baking soda, and salt. In a medium bowl, whisk together the buttermilk, oil, eggs, vinegar, and vanilla.

4. Slowly add the buttermilk mixture to the flour mixture, whisking until combined. Add the food coloring and fold into the batter.

5. Spoon 3 cups of the batter into the Bundt pan. Carefully spoon the cream cheese filling over the batter without touching the sides of the pan. Spoon the remaining batter over the cream cheese mixture. Bake for 45 to 55 minutes or until the cake is lightly browned. Let the cake cool in the pan for 10 to 15 minutes, then invert onto a wire rack and let cool completely. Transfer the cake to a serving plate.

6. *For the cream cheese glaze:* Combine the cream cheese, confectioners' sugar, sour cream, and vanilla and whisk until smooth and thick.

7. Drizzle the glaze over the cake and let it set. Slice and serve.

Neapolitan Bundt Cake

Yield: Serves 12 | Prep Time: 20 minutes | Cook Time: 35 to 45 minutes

Growing up, it was always a treat to find a container of Neapolitan ice cream in the freezer. It looked so simple and idyllic with the white paired against the brown and pink. This cake, with its soft, pleasing color palette, is an elegant addition to any party.

INGREDIENTS

All-purpose flour for the pan

1 (15.25-ounce) box yellow cake mix

¼ cup vegetable oil

3 large eggs

1 teaspoon vanilla bean paste or vanilla extract

8 drops red liquid food coloring

¼ cup chocolate syrup or hot fudge sauce (see Notes)

1 tablespoon cocoa powder

Confectioners' sugar for dusting

DIRECTIONS

1. Preheat the oven to 350°F. Grease and flour a 12-cup Bundt pan.

2. Using a hand mixer or a stand mixer fitted with the paddle attachment, combine the cake mix, oil, eggs, vanilla, and 1 cup water. Beat on low speed for 30 seconds, then increase the speed to medium and beat for 2 minutes.

3. Divide the batter into 3 equal portions. Pour one portion into the Bundt pan. Stir the red food coloring into another portion of batter. Spoon over the first layer of batter.

4. Stir the chocolate syrup and the cocoa powder into the last portion of batter. Carefully spread into the pan. Do not swirl!

5. Bake for 35 to 45 minutes or until a toothpick inserted in the center comes out clean. Let the cake cool in the pan for 10 minutes, then invert onto a wire rack and let cool completely. Dust the cake with confectioners' sugar. Slice and serve.

NOTES

If you're using fudge topping instead of chocolate syrup, microwave for 15 to 20 seconds on high before adding to the batter.

Pink Lemonade Bundt Cakes

Yield: Serves 12 | Prep Time: 15 minutes | Cook Time: 25 to 30 minutes

The pink lemonade concentrate adds a sweet-tart flavor to both the cakes and the glaze, while the colorful sprinkles make it perfectly party-worthy. Mini Bundt pans create individual cakes, which are lots of fun for a kid's birthday party.

INGREDIENTS

Cake

All-purpose flour for the pan

1 (16.5-ounce) box lemon cake mix

1 (3.4-ounce) box lemon instant pudding mix

4 large eggs

½ cup frozen pink lemonade concentrate, thawed

½ cup milk

⅓ cup vegetable oil

1–2 drops red or pink liquid food coloring

Glaze

1 cup confectioners' sugar

3–4 tablespoons frozen pink lemonade concentrate, thawed

1–2 drops red or pink liquid food coloring

Rainbow sprinkles for decorating

DIRECTIONS

1. Preheat the oven to 350°F. Grease and flour two 6-cavity mini Bundt pans.

2. *For the cake:* In a large bowl, combine the cake mix, pudding mix, eggs, lemonade concentrate, milk, oil, and food coloring. Blend until smooth.

3. Pour the batter into each mini Bundt cavity three-quarters full.

4. Bake for 25 to 30 minutes until the cakes are golden and a toothpick inserted in the center comes out clean.

5. Let the cakes cool in the pans for 10 minutes, then invert onto a wire rack and let cool completely.

6. *For the glaze:* Combine the confectioners' sugar with enough lemonade concentrate to make a pourable consistency. Stir in food coloring to achieve the desired shade of pink. Add an extra drop for a darker shade. Drizzle the glaze over the cakes and top with the sprinkles. Transfer to individual dessert plates and serve.

NOTES

If you'd like to make one large cake instead of individual cakes, grease and flour a 12-cup Bundt pan. Make the batter as directed, then bake the cake for 50 minutes to 1 hour. Let the cake cool in the pan for 10 minutes, before turning it out onto a wire rack and letting cool completely.

Classic Buttery Pound Cake

Yield: Serves 12 | Prep Time: 20 minutes | Cook Time: 25 to 30 minutes

The name "pound cake" comes from the way the recipe used to be made: it called for one pound each of butter, sugar, eggs, and flour. This simple formula made it easy to remember. Pound cake recipes have become more sophisticated over the years. This version uses sour cream to add to the density, but it's just as tasty as ever.

INGREDIENTS

3 cups all-purpose flour, plus extra for the pan

16 tablespoons (2 sticks) unsalted butter, softened

½ cup vegetable shortening

3 cups granulated sugar

5 large eggs

½ teaspoon kosher salt

½ teaspoon baking powder

½ cup milk

½ cup sour cream

1 teaspoon vanilla bean paste or vanilla extract

1 teaspoon grated lemon zest

Confectioners' sugar for dusting

DIRECTIONS

1. Preheat the oven to 350°F. Grease and flour two 6-cavity mini Bundt pans.

2. Using a hand mixer or a stand mixer fitted with the paddle attachment, beat the butter and shortening on medium speed until fluffy. Add the sugar gradually until fully mixed in. Beat in the eggs, one at a time. In a medium bowl, whisk together the flour, salt, and baking powder. In a measuring cup, combine the milk, sour cream, and vanilla.

3. On low speed, add the flour mixture to the butter mixture in 3 batches, alternating with the sour cream mixture in 2 batches, beating until combined. Stir in the lemon zest.

4. Fill each mini Bundt cavity three-quarters full.

5. Bake for 25 to 30 minutes until the cakes are golden and a toothpick inserted in the center comes out clean.

6. Let the cakes cool in the pans for 10 minutes, then invert onto a wire rack and let cool completely.

7. Transfer to individual dessert plates, dust with confectioners' sugar, and serve.

NOTES

If you'd like to make one large cake instead of individual cakes, grease and flour a 12-cup Bundt pan. Make the batter as directed, then bake the cake for 1½ hours. Let the cake cool in the pan for 10 minutes, before turning it out onto a wire rack and letting cool completely.

Cinnamon Roll Pound Cake

Yield: Serves 18 | Prep Time: 25 minutes | Cook Time: 50 minutes to 1 hour

The combination of cinnamon and cream cheese reminds me of Sunday mornings with my friends. We'd wake up late and head to our favorite brunch spot and gorge on sticky cinnamon rolls for the table before spending the day at a museum or the movies. These pound cakes take that leisurely Sunday morning essence to provide one cake for breakfast and another for dessert!

INGREDIENTS

Cake

16 tablespoons (2 sticks) unsalted butter, softened

3¼ cups granulated sugar

1 cup sour cream

3 tablespoons heavy cream

1 teaspoon vanilla bean paste or vanilla extract

6 large eggs

3 cups all-purpose flour

½ teaspoon baking soda

1 tablespoon ground cinnamon

Glaze

1½ cups confectioners' sugar

2 ounces cream cheese, room temperature

2 tablespoons unsalted butter, softened

¼ cup heavy cream

1 teaspoon vanilla bean paste or vanilla extract

DIRECTIONS

1. Preheat the oven to 350°F. Grease two 9 × 5-inch loaf pans. Line the pans with parchment paper, leaving an overhang on the long sides. Grease the parchment paper.

2. *For the cake:* Using a hand mixer or a stand mixer fitted with the paddle attachment, beat the butter on medium speed for 1 to 2 minutes until smooth and creamy. Add 3 cups of the sugar and beat until light and fluffy.

3. Beat in the sour cream, then the cream and vanilla. Beat in the eggs, one at a time.

4. In a small bowl, whisk together the flour and baking soda. On low speed, add the flour mixture to the butter mixture, beating until just combined.

5. In a small bowl mix the remaining ¼ cup sugar with the cinnamon. Divide one-third of the batter between the 2 loaf pans. Sprinkle half of the cinnamon sugar mixture over the batter. Repeat with another third of the batter, then the remaining cinnamon sugar, and top with the remaining batter.

6. Bake for 50 minutes to 1 hour or until the cakes are golden and a toothpick inserted in the center comes out clean.

7. Let the cakes cool in the pans. Using the parchment paper, lift the cakes out of the pans and transfer to a baking sheet.

8. *For the glaze:* Beat the confectioners' sugar, cream cheese, butter, cream, and vanilla until smooth and pourable. Pour the glaze over the cooled cakes. Slice and serve.

Brownie Butter Cake

Yield: Serves 6 to 8 │ Prep Time: 25 minutes │ Cook Time: 45 to 55 minutes

The combination of dark chocolate and espresso gives this cake a mix of bitterness and sweetness. The dark chocolate and coconut oil glaze is something I've used on top of other desserts like cookies, brownies, and cupcakes, and it adds a rich, restaurant-worthy touch.

INGREDIENTS

Brownie Layer

5 ounces bittersweet dark chocolate, chopped

4 tablespoons unsalted butter

¼ cup packed light brown sugar

1 large egg

¼ cup all-purpose flour

¼ teaspoon espresso powder

Butter Layer

8 tablespoons (1 stick) unsalted butter

½ cup sugar

2 large eggs

1 cup all-purpose flour

¼ teaspoon baking powder

3½ tablespoons milk

½ teaspoon vanilla bean paste or vanilla extract

Glaze

½ cup bittersweet dark chocolate chips

1 teaspoon coconut oil

DIRECTIONS

1. Preheat the oven to 350°F. Grease a 9 × 5-inch loaf pan. Line the pan with parchment paper, leaving an overhang on the long sides.

2. *For the brownie layer:* Melt the chocolate and butter over low heat or in a microwave. Let cool, then stir in the brown sugar. Add the egg and whisk until blended. Fold in the flour and espresso powder. Pour the batter into the loaf pan and bake for 15 minutes.

3. *For the butter layer:* Beat the butter with the sugar until fluffy. Add the eggs, one at a time. Fold in the flour and baking powder. Stir in the milk and vanilla and mix until combined.

4. Carefully spread the butter cake batter over the brownie layer. Bake for 25 to 30 minutes or until the cake is golden and a toothpick inserted in the center comes out clean.

5. Let the cake cool in the pan for 10 minutes. Using the parchment as a handle, transfer the cake to a wire rack and let cool completely.

6. *For the glaze:* Microwave the chocolate chips with the coconut oil for 1 to 2 minutes, stirring every 20 seconds until the chocolate is melted. Drizzle over the cooled cake. Slice and serve.

Italian Lemon Mini Pound Cakes

Yield: 12 mini Bundt cakes | Prep Time: 20 minutes | Cook Time: 25 to 30 minutes for mini Bundt cakes

These little cakes, with their double layer of glaze and frosting and dense, lemony cake, remind me of doughnuts. The bright citrus flavor makes them an ideal pick-me-up for a gloomy, rainy day.

INGREDIENTS

Cake

3 cups all-purpose flour, plus extra for the pans

1 teaspoon baking powder

¼ teaspoon kosher salt

16 tablespoons (2 sticks) unsalted butter, softened

2 cups granulated sugar

3 large eggs

½ cup sour cream

¼ cup lemon juice

2 tablespoons grated lemon zest

1 teaspoon vanilla bean paste or vanilla extract

1 teaspoon limoncello liqueur

½ cup buttermilk

Glaze

1½ cups confectioners' sugar

2 tablespoons lemon juice

1 tablespoon limoncello liqueur

Lemon Mascarpone Topping

4 ounces mascarpone cheese, room temperature

1 tablespoon grated lemon zest plus ¼ cup lemon juice, plus extra zest for garnish

1 teaspoon limoncello liqueur

2 cups confectioners' sugar

DIRECTIONS

1. Preheat the oven to 325°F. Grease and flour two 6-cavity mini Bundt pans.

2. *For the cake:* In a large bowl, whisk together the flour, baking powder and salt.

3. Using a hand mixer or a stand mixer fitted with the paddle attachment, beat the butter on medium speed for 1 minute, then add the sugar and beat until light and creamy. Add the eggs one at a time, beating well after each addition. Beat in the sour cream, lemon juice, lemon zest, vanilla, and limoncello.

4. On low speed, add half of the flour mixture, followed by the buttermilk, and then the remaining flour mixture, beating to combine. Fill each mini Bundt cavity three-quarters full.

5. Bake for 25 to 30 minutes or until the cakes are golden and a toothpick inserted in the center comes out clean.

6. Let the cakes cool in the pans for 10 minutes, then invert onto a wire rack and let cool completely.

7. *For the glaze:* Whisk the confectioners' sugar with the lemon juice and limoncello. Drizzle the glaze over the cake(s).

8. *For the lemon-mascarpone topping:* Beat the mascarpone cheese with the lemon zest, lemon juice, limoncello, and confectioners' sugar until smooth.

9. After the cakes have cooled, drizzle the mascarpone frosting over the cakes. Sprinkle with lemon zest. Serve.

NOTES

If you'd like to make one large cake instead of individual cakes, grease and flour a 12-cup Bundt pan. Make the batter as directed, then bake the cake for 1 hour 10 minutes to 1 hour 20 minutes. Let the cake cool in the pan for 10 minutes, before turning it out onto a wire rack and letting cool completely. Make the frosting and drizzle it on the cake as directed.

Coconut Pound Cake

Yield: Serves 8 to 12 | Prep Time: 20 minutes |
Cook Time: 1 hour to 1 hour 5 minutes for large loaf, 45 to 50 minutes for mini loaf

While coconut itself is sweet, smooth, and comforting, it's the hint of lime zest that gives this recipe an edgy twist. I make this cake around Easter, and I never wind up with any leftovers. I like to use the large loaf to serve to family and friends and keep the smaller one for myself!

INGREDIENTS

Cakes

16 tablespoons (2 sticks) unsalted butter, softened

1¾ cups sugar

3 large eggs

2 teaspoons coconut extract

1 teaspoon grated lime zest

½ teaspoon vanilla bean paste or vanilla extract

2½ cups all-purpose flour

2 teaspoons baking powder

1 teaspoon kosher salt

¾ cup buttermilk

1 cup sweetened shredded coconut

Glaze

1½ cups confectioners' sugar

2 tablespoons heavy cream

1 teaspoon vanilla bean paste or vanilla extract

1 teaspoon coconut extract

1 cup sweetened shredded coconut

DIRECTIONS

1. Preheat the oven to 350°F. Grease and flour one 9 × 5-inch loaf pan and one 5 × 3-inch mini loaf pan.

2. *For the cakes:* Using a hand mixer or a stand mixer fitted with the paddle attachment, beat the butter with the sugar on medium speed until light and fluffy. Add the eggs, one at a time, beating well after each addition. Beat in the coconut extract, lime zest, and vanilla.

3. In a large bowl, whisk together the flour, baking powder, and salt.

4. On low speed, add the flour mixture to the butter mixture in 3 batches, alternating with the buttermilk in 2 batches, beating until combined. Fold in the coconut.

5. Pour the batter into the loaf pans. Bake until the cake is golden and a toothpick inserted in the center comes out clean, 1 hour to 1 hour 5 minutes for the large loaf and 45 to 50 minutes for the mini loaf.

6. Let the cakes cool in the pans for 10 to 15 minutes, then turn out onto a wire rack and let cool completely.

7. *For the glaze:* Whisk together the confectioners' sugar, cream, vanilla, and coconut extract until smooth and pourable. Drizzle the glaze over the cakes and top with the coconut. Slice and serve.

Southern Pecan Pound Cake

Yield: Serves 12 to 14 | Prep Time: 45 minutes | Cook Time: 1 hour to 1 hour 10 minutes

When I first started baking my own cakes, I got frustrated any time I tried adding nuts or chocolate chips into the batter because they'd inevitably sink to the bottom instead of staying evenly sprinkled throughout. When I was in culinary school, I learned to mix the nuts or chocolate chips with flour before adding them to the batter to prevent them from sinking to the bottom of the cake. I've used this trick ever since!

INGREDIENTS

Cake

2¼ cups plus 1 tablespoon all-purpose flour, plus extra for the pan

1 cup pecan halves, broken into ¼-inch pieces and toasted

1 teaspoon baking powder

¼ teaspoon kosher salt

16 tablespoons (2 sticks) unsalted butter, softened

1⅓ cups sugar

5 large eggs

1 teaspoon vanilla bean paste or vanilla extract

1 teaspoon rum extract

⅓ cup sour cream

Topping

½ cup pecan halves

1 tablespoon sugar

DIRECTIONS

1. Preheat the oven to 325°F. Grease and flour a 16-cup tube pan.

2. *For the cake:* Toss the pecans with 1 tablespoon of the flour and set aside.

3. In a medium bowl, whisk together the remaining 2¼ cups flour, the baking powder, and salt.

4. Using a hand mixer or a stand mixer fitted with the paddle attachment, beat the butter on medium speed for 1 to 2 minutes, then slowly add the sugar and beat until the mixture is fluffy. Scrape down the bowl. Add the eggs, one at a time, and beat well after each addition. Add the vanilla and rum extract.

5. On low speed, add about half of the flour mixture, then the sour cream, and then the remaining flour, beating until combined. Scrape down the sides of the bowl to make sure the batter is fully mixed. Carefully fold in the pecans. Spoon the batter into the tube pan.

6. *For the topping:* Sprinkle the pecans and then the sugar over the batter.

7. Bake for 1 hour to 1 hour 10 minutes or until the cake is golden and a toothpick inserted in the center comes out clean.

8. Let the cake cool in the pan for 15 minutes. Remove the cake from the pan to a wire rack to cool completely. Slice and serve.

Chocolate Pound Cake

Yield: Serves 8 | Prep Time: 15 minutes, plus 1½ to 2 hours chill time | Cook Time: 45 to 55 minutes

While the density of pound cakes is usually achieved by using a lot of butter, in this cake I opted for sour cream and buttermilk to stand in for some of the butter. Their moisture makes for a creamier cake, which, with the addition of cocoa, reminds me of a steaming mug of hot chocolate.

INGREDIENTS

Cake

8 tablespoons (1 stick) unsalted butter, softened

¾ cup sugar

2 large eggs

1 teaspoon vanilla bean paste or vanilla extract

1 tablespoon espresso powder

½ cup sour cream

¼ cup buttermilk

1 cup plus 2 tablespoons all-purpose flour

½ cup cocoa powder

½ teaspoon kosher salt

½ teaspoon baking soda

Ganache

¾ cup heavy cream

6 ounces bittersweet dark chocolate, chopped

DIRECTIONS

1. Preheat the oven to 325°F. Lightly grease a 9 × 5-inch loaf pan. Line the pan with parchment paper, leaving an overhang on the long sides.

2. *For the cake:* Using a hand mixer or a stand mixer fitted with the paddle attachment, beat the butter on medium speed for 1 minute, then add the sugar and beat until fluffy. Beat in the eggs, one at a time. Add the vanilla and espresso and beat to combine.

3. In a small bowl, whisk together the sour cream and buttermilk. In another small bowl, whisk together the flour, cocoa, salt, and baking soda. On low speed, add the flour mixture to the butter mixture in 3 batches, alternating with the sour cream mixture in 2 batches; beat until blended.

4. Pour the batter into the loaf pan and bake for 45 to 55 minutes or until a toothpick inserted in the center comes out clean. Be careful not to overbake the cake. Transfer to a wire rack and let the cake cool completely in the pan.

5. *For the ganache:* Heat the cream in the microwave or on the stovetop just until simmering. Place the chocolate in a heatproof bowl, pour the hot cream over the chocolate, and let stand for 2 to 3 minutes, then stir until smooth. Let the mixture sit for about 5 minutes before pouring over the cooled cake. Refrigerate the cake for 1½ to 2 hours to firm up.

6. Carefully lift the cake from the pan using the parchment paper. Slice and serve.

Cherry 7UP Pound Cake

Yield: Serves 12 to 16 | Prep Time: 20 minutes | Cook Time: 1 hour 10 minutes to 1 hour 25 minutes

One of my favorite treats as a kid was drinking a kiddie cocktail, and Cherry 7UP was the next closest thing. This cake version has that sweet bubbly sensation we all love with the cozy comfort of old-fashioned pound cake.

INGREDIENTS

Cake

All-purpose flour for the pan

24 tablespoons (3 sticks) unsalted butter, softened

3 cups granulated sugar

1 teaspoon kosher salt

5 large eggs

1 teaspoon vanilla bean paste or vanilla extract

1 teaspoon grated lemon zest

3 cups cake flour, sifted

½ cup Cherry 7UP

½ cup maraschino cherries, patted dry

Glazes

2 cups confectioners' sugar

3 tablespoons maraschino cherry juice

2 tablespoons heavy cream

DIRECTIONS

1. Preheat the oven to 315°F. Grease and flour a 10-cup Bundt pan.

2. *For the cake:* Using a hand mixer or a stand mixer fitted with the paddle attachment, beat the butter on medium speed for 2 to 3 minutes until light and fluffy. Add the sugar and salt and beat for 6 to 7 minutes until fluffy and very light, scraping down the bowl a few times. Add the eggs, one at a time, beating until incorporated. Add the vanilla and lemon zest. Reduce the speed to low and add the cake flour gradually, beating until combined. Add the Cherry 7UP and mix in, then carefully fold in the cherries. Pour the batter into the Bundt pan.

3. Bake for 1 hour 10 minutes to 1 hour 25 minutes or until the cake is golden and a toothpick inserted in the center comes out clean. Let the cake cool in the pan for 10 minutes, then invert onto a serving plate. Let cool completely.

4. *For the glazes:* Place 1 cup of the confectioners' sugar in each of 2 bowls. To 1 bowl, add the cherry juice and whisk until smooth. To the other bowl, add the cream and whisk until smooth. Pour the white glaze over the cake, then drizzle with the cherry glaze. Slice and serve.

3

Old-Fashioned Cakes

Cakes have been the stars of the dessert table for generations. Whether Grandma was making her special Jimmy Cake (page 50) for the neighborhood bake sale or teenagers were meeting up with friends after school to enjoy a slice of Dandy Diner Dream Cake (page 58) while listening to Elvis's latest hit on the jukebox, cakes made every gathering a celebration. These vintage favorites are here to stay.

Grandma's Famous Jimmy Cake

Yield: Serves 12 | Prep Time: 20 minutes | Cook Time: 50 minutes to 1 hour

"Jimmy" is just an old-fashioned word for sprinkles—and boy, does this recipe have a lot of those! I used chocolate sprinkles for my version, but if you prefer a single color or rainbow sprinkles, feel free to substitute those.

INGREDIENTS

Cake

4 large egg whites

½ cup vegetable shortening or coconut oil

8 tablespoons (1 stick) unsalted butter, softened

2 cups confectioners' sugar

4 large egg yolks

1 cup cold coffee

1 teaspoon espresso powder

1 teaspoon vanilla bean paste or vanilla extract

2 cups all-purpose flour

½ teaspoon kosher salt

2 teaspoons baking powder

1 cup chocolate sprinkles

Glaze

2 tablespoons milk or heavy cream, plus extra if needed

1 teaspoon espresso powder

2 cups confectioners' sugar

Chocolate sprinkles for decorating

DIRECTIONS

1. Preheat the oven to 325°F. Grease a 16-cup tube pan.

2. *For the cake:* Using a hand mixer or stand mixer fitted with the whisk attachment, beat the egg whites on medium speed until the peaks stand straight up when the whisk is removed. Transfer to a separate bowl and set aside.

3. Switch to the paddle attachment, put the shortening and butter in the empty mixer bowl, and beat on medium speed until light. Add the confectioners' sugar and beat until combined. Scrape down the bowl. Beat in the egg yolks, coffee, espresso powder, and vanilla. On low speed, beat in the flour, salt, and baking powder. Stir in the sprinkles. Fold in the beaten egg whites.

4. Pour the batter into the tube pan and bake for 50 minutes to 1 hour or until the cake is golden and a toothpick inserted in the center comes out clean.

5. Let the cake cool in the pan for 10 minutes, then carefully remove and place on a serving plate to cool completely.

6. *For the glaze:* In a medium bowl, whisk together the milk and espresso powder. Whisk in the confectioners' sugar until smooth, adding more milk as needed for a pourable glaze.

7. Drizzle the glaze over the cake and decorate with sprinkles. Slice and serve.

1970s Harvey Wallbanger Cake

Yield: Serves 10 to 12 | Prep Time: 10 minutes | Cook Time: 45 to 50 minutes

The Harvey Wallbanger is a classic cocktail that combines vodka, orange juice, and Galliano. This sweet cake version packs a double whammy with the cocktail flavor in both the cake itself and the citrus glaze.

INGREDIENTS

Cake

All-purpose flour for the pan

1 (18.75-ounce) box yellow cake mix (see Notes)

1 cup vegetable oil

2 teaspoons grated orange zest plus ¾ cup orange juice

4 large eggs

¼ cup Galliano liqueur

¼ cup vodka

1 (3.4-ounce) box vanilla instant pudding mix

1 teaspoon vanilla bean paste or vanilla extract

Glaze

1 cup confectioners' sugar

1 teaspoon grated orange zest plus 1 tablespoon orange juice

1 tablespoon Galliano liqueur

1 teaspoon vodka

DIRECTIONS

1. Preheat the oven to 350°F. Grease and flour a 9-cup Bundt pan.

2. *For the cake:* Using a hand mixer or a stand mixer fitted with the paddle attachment, beat the cake mix, oil, orange zest and juice, eggs, Galliano, vodka, pudding mix, and vanilla on medium speed for 3 minutes. Pour the batter into the Bundt pan and gently tap to release air bubbles.

3. Bake for 45 to 50 minutes or until the cake is golden and a toothpick inserted in the center comes out clean. Let the cake cool in the pan for 10 minutes. Invert the cake onto a serving plate to cool completely.

4. *For the glaze:* In a small bowl, whisk together the confectioners' sugar, orange zest and juice, Galliano, and vodka. Drizzle the glaze over the warm cake. Let the glaze set before slicing and serving.

NOTES

Be sure to use 18.75 ounces of cake mix—the recipe won't work with less. If needed, buy two boxes to reach the required amount.

Lemon Crazy Cake

Yield: Serves 9 to 12 | Prep Time: 5 minutes | Cook Time: 35 minutes

Crazy cake was a recipe that took on many forms during the Great Depression. Because certain ingredients were so expensive, cooks needed to get creative and find ways to enjoy their favorite recipes without using baking essentials like eggs, milk, and butter. Instead, the white vinegar reacts with the baking soda to lift the batter and provide that cakey texture we know and love.

INGREDIENTS

Cake

1½ cups plus 3 tablespoons all-purpose flour

1 cup granulated sugar

1 teaspoon baking soda

½ teaspoon kosher salt

1 tablespoon grated lemon zest

5 tablespoons vegetable oil

1 teaspoon vanilla bean paste or vanilla extract

1 teaspoon lemon extract

1 teaspoon white vinegar

Frosting

8 tablespoons (1 stick) unsalted butter, softened

2 cups confectioners' sugar

2 tablespoons heavy cream

2 teaspoons lemon juice

½ teaspoon vanilla bean paste or vanilla extract

DIRECTIONS

1. Preheat the oven to 350°F. Lightly grease an 8-inch square baking dish.

2. *For the cake:* Place the flour, sugar, baking soda, salt, and lemon zest in the baking dish and stir until combined.

3. Make 1 large depression and two small ones in the dry ingredients. Pour the oil into the large depression, the vanilla and lemon extract into one of the small depressions, and the vinegar into the other small depression. Pour 1 cup of water over all and stir until combined and smooth.

4. Bake for 35 minutes or until the cake is golden and a toothpick inserted in the center comes out clean. Let the cake cool completely in the pan.

5. *For the frosting:* Using a hand mixer or stand mixer fitted with the whisk attachment, whip the butter, confectioners' sugar, cream, lemon juice, and vanilla until fluffy. Spread over the cooled cake. Slice and serve.

Grandmother's Lazy Daisy Cake

Yield: Serves 9 | Prep Time: 25 minutes | Cook Time: 45 to 55 minutes

This lazy daisy cake works well when you're in a rush. Once you make the oatmeal, it only takes another five minutes to combine all the ingredients. Then just pop it in the oven to get a simple, made-from-scratch dessert.

INGREDIENTS

Cake

1 cup quick-cooking oats

1¼ cups boiling water

8 tablespoons (1 stick) unsalted butter, softened

1 cup granulated sugar

1 cup packed light brown sugar

2 large eggs

1 teaspoon vanilla bean paste or vanilla extract

1½ cups all-purpose flour, plus extra for the pan

1 teaspoon baking soda

¾ teaspoon ground cinnamon

½ teaspoon kosher salt

¼ teaspoon ground nutmeg

Caramel Frosting

1½ cups packed light brown sugar

¾ cup heavy cream

2 tablespoons unsalted butter

½ teaspoon vanilla bean paste or vanilla extract

½ cup shredded sweetened coconut

½ cup chopped pecans

DIRECTIONS

1. Preheat the oven to 350°F. Grease and flour a 9-inch square baking dish.

2. *For the cake:* Place the oatmeal in a small bowl and pour the boiling water over the oats. Cover and let stand for 20 minutes.

3. Using a hand mixer or a stand mixer fitted with the paddle attachment, beat the butter for 1 to 2 minutes on medium speed until light. Add the granulated sugar and brown sugar a bit at a time, beating until incorporated and the mixture is light and fluffy. Add the eggs, vanilla, and oats and beat until combined. On low speed, beat in the flour, baking soda, cinnamon, salt, and nutmeg until combined.

4. Pour into the baking dish. Bake for 45 to 55 minutes or until the cake is golden and a toothpick inserted in the center comes out clean. Let cool for 10 minutes in the pan. Then invert onto a serving plate to cool completely.

5. *For the caramel frosting:* In a large saucepan, combine the brown sugar and cream. Cook over medium-low heat until the mixture comes to a low boil. Continue to cook until the mixture is thickened, about 10 minutes, stirring constantly.

6. Remove from the heat and stir in the butter and vanilla. Let the frosting cool. It will thicken more as it cools. With a wire whisk, beat the frosting to a smooth consistency and spread over the top of the cake. Sprinkle with the coconut and pecans. Slice and serve.

Dandy Diner Dream Cake

Yield: Serves 12 | Prep Time: 1 hour plus 1¼ hours chill time | Cook Time: 25 to 35 minutes

Whenever I think of diners, I always imagine those glass display cases filled with the most decadent pies and cakes you can imagine. These were the kind of treats you aspired to make.

INGREDIENTS

Cake

1 (16.25-ounce) box white cake mix

Vegetable oil as needed for the cake mix

Eggs as needed for the cake mix

¾ cup bittersweet dark chocolate chips

Peanut Butter Mousse

¾ cup heavy cream

8 ounces cream cheese, cut into cubes

1 cup confectioners' sugar

¾ cup creamy peanut butter

1 tablespoon vanilla bean paste or vanilla extract

Whipped Cream Frosting

2 cups heavy cream

¼ cup confectioners' sugar

2 teaspoons vanilla bean paste or vanilla extract

Peanut and Cherry Decoration

½ cup chopped roasted peanuts

½ cup turbinado sugar

8 maraschino cherries, patted dry

DIRECTIONS

1. Preheat the oven and prepare the cake mix according to package directions. Grease two 8-inch round cake pans. Line the pans with parchment paper and grease the parchment. Stir in the dark chocolate chips. Pour into the pans and bake according to package directions. Let cool completely.

2. *For the peanut butter mousse:* Using a hand mixer or stand mixer fitted with the whisk attachment, whip the cream on medium-high speed for 2 to 3 minutes or until firm peaks form. Transfer to a separate bowl. Add the cream cheese, confectioners' sugar, peanut butter, and vanilla to the empty bowl and whip until light and fluffy, 3 to 4 minutes. Using a spatula, fold the whipped cream into the peanut butter mixture until combined. Cover and refrigerate until ready to use.

3. *For the whipped cream frosting:* Using a clean, chilled bowl, whip the cream and confectioners' sugar on medium-high speed until firm peaks form. Reduce the speed to low and mix in the vanilla bean paste.

4. Place 1 cake layer on a serving plate. Spread the peanut butter mousse filling evenly over the cake and place the second cake layer on top. Fit a pastry bag with a star tip and put about ½ cup of the whipped cream frosting in the bag. Spread the remaining whipped cream frosting on the top and sides. Pipe rosettes on top. Refrigerate for 1 hour.

5. *For the peanut sugar coating:* Combine the peanuts and sugar in a small bowl, and carefully pat around the sides of the cake. Top with the maraschino cherries. Slice and serve.

NOTES

The peanut butter mousse filling can be made ahead and refrigerated.

Pineapple Upside-Down Cake

Yield: Serves 8 to 10 | Prep Time: 15 minutes plus 30 minutes chill time | Cook Time: 40 minutes

Upside-down cakes were developed centuries ago when much of the cooking was done in cast-iron skillets. Cake batter was poured on top of fruit and sugar and placed over an open fire to cook. To get the cake out, it was easiest to just flip the whole thing upside down! Pineapple upside-down cake was particularly popular during the '50s and '60s since it was such a pretty, colorful cake to show off to guests.

INGREDIENTS

8 tablespoons (1 stick) unsalted butter

¾ cup packed light brown sugar

1 (20-ounce) can pineapple slices (about 8 slices)

17 maraschino cherries

1 cup all-purpose flour

¾ cup granulated sugar

2 teaspoons baking powder

½ teaspoon ground cardamom

¼ teaspoon kosher salt

½ cup buttermilk

⅓ cup sour cream

1 large egg

3 tablespoons vegetable oil

1 teaspoon vanilla bean paste or vanilla extract

1 teaspoon rum extract

DIRECTIONS

1. Preheat the oven to 350°F. Put the butter in a small bowl and melt in the microwave, about 1 minute. Pour the melted butter into a 9-inch round cake pan. Sprinkle the brown sugar over the butter. Place 5 whole pineapple slices in the pan. (See photo.) Halve 2 slices of pineapple and place them between the whole slices. Place 1 cherry in the center of each whole pineapple slice, each half slice center cutout, and in between the whole and half slices.

2. In a large bowl, whisk together the flour, granulated sugar, baking powder, cardamom, and salt. In a small bowl, whisk together the buttermilk, sour cream, egg, oil, vanilla, and rum extract. Add the buttermilk mixture to the flour mixture, folding in with a spatula just until combined. Do not overmix.

3. Carefully pour the batter over the pineapple, filling about ¾ full. Place the pan on a baking sheet to catch any drips.

4. Bake for 40 minutes or until the cake is set and golden. Transfer the pan to a wire rack and let cool for 30 minutes. Invert the pan onto a serving plate. Slice and serve.

The Best Angel Food Cake

Yield: Serves 10 to 12 | Prep Time: 20 minutes | Cook Time: 35 minutes

You may have seen cream of tartar used in recipes for meringue toppings. When mixed with egg whites, the cream of tartar helps the meringue form into stiff peaks and maintain its shape, even under high heat. A similar science is applied here for angel food cake, where the combination of cream of tartar and egg whites helps the cake maintain its buoyancy.

INGREDIENTS

1¾ cups sugar

1 cup cake flour

¼ teaspoon kosher salt

12 large egg whites (1½ cups), room temperature

⅓ cup warm water (110°F)

1 teaspoon orange extract

1½ teaspoons cream of tartar

Whipped cream for serving

Assorted fresh berries for serving

DIRECTIONS

1. Preheat the oven to 350°F.

2. In a food processor, pulse the sugar until very fine. In a small bowl, whisk together the flour, salt, and half of the sugar.

3. In a stand mixer fitted with the whisk attachment, combine the egg whites, water, orange extract, and cream of tartar on medium speed for 2 minutes. Gradually add the remaining sugar, beating until medium peaks are formed. Sprinkle some of the flour over the egg white mixture and gently stir in by hand. Gradually add the remaining flour mixture, stirring gently until it is incorporated.

4. Spoon the batter into an ungreased 16-cup angel food cake pan. Bake for 35 minutes or until the cake is golden and springs back when touched.

5. Invert the cake pan and let the cake cool completely in the pan. Carefully remove the cake from the pan and set on a serving plate. Slice and serve with whipped cream and berries.

Creamy Lemon Angel Cake

Yield: Serves 10 | Prep Time: 20 to 25 minutes | Cook Time: 15 to 20 minutes

Cake flour has less protein than all-purpose flour, which means cakes made with it are softer and more tender—exactly how I'd describe this Creamy Lemon Angel Cake.

INGREDIENTS

Cake

9 large egg whites, room temperature

1 teaspoon vanilla bean paste or vanilla extract

¾ teaspoon cream of tartar

1 cup plus 2 tablespoons granulated sugar

¾ cup cake flour

Filling

1 cup granulated sugar

3 tablespoons cornstarch

1 large egg

1 tablespoon grated lemon zest plus ¼ cup lemon juice

1 cup pre-made whipped cream

Confectioners' sugar

DIRECTIONS

1. Preheat the oven to 350°F. Lightly coat a 10 × 15-inch jelly-roll pan with cooking spray. Line the pan with parchment paper, leaving a small overhang on the short sides of the pan. Spray the parchment with cooking spray.

2. *For the cake:* Using a hand mixer or a stand mixer fitted with the whisk attachment, whip the egg whites, vanilla, and cream of tartar on medium speed until soft peaks form. Increase the speed to high and add the sugar a little at a time, whiping until stiff peaks form. Fold in the flour.

3. Spread the batter into the baking pan and bake for 15 to 20 minutes or until the cake is set and springs back when touched. Let it cool for 5 to 7 minutes.

4. Carefully lift the cake out of the pan using the parchment paper.

5. Roll up the cake jelly roll–style with the parchment paper, starting with the short end. Let the cake cool completely on a wire rack.

6. *For the filling:* In a medium saucepan, combine the sugar and cornstarch. Whisk in 1 cup water until smooth. Cook and stir over medium-high heat until the mixture is thick. Cook for 1 minute. Remove from the heat.

7. In a small bowl, beat the egg. Add some of the hot mixture to the egg to temper. Add the egg mixture back into the pan and, stirring, bring back to a low boil. Remove from the heat.

8. Add the lemon zest and juice. Let cool and then fold in the whipped cream.

9. Carefully unroll the cake using the parchment. Spread the filling to within ½ inch of the edges. Reroll the cake, peeling off the parchment as you roll. Carefully place the cake roll on a serving plate. Sprinkle the top with confectioners' sugar. Slice and serve.

Victoria Sponge Cake

Yield: Serves 10 | Prep Time: 20 minutes | Cook Time: 20 to 25 minutes

Victoria sponge cake is the poster child for teatime desserts. Teatime was popularized in the 1800s after Anna, the Duchess of Bedford and one of Queen Victoria's ladies-in-waiting, felt she needed a snack around 4 p.m. to tide her over until the fashionably late dinners of the time. Friends began to join her for mid-afternoon snacks, and the trend spread. This cake was one of the queen's favorite sweets.

INGREDIENTS

4 tablespoons unsalted butter, melted, plus 16 tablespoons (2 sticks) unsalted butter, softened

1 cup granulated sugar

4 large eggs

2 teaspoons vanilla bean paste or vanilla extract

1 teaspoon grated orange zest

1 cup all-purpose flour

1½ teaspoons baking powder

½ teaspoon kosher salt

1½ cups heavy cream

¾ cup raspberry jam

1 pint fresh raspberries

Confectioners' sugar for dusting

DIRECTIONS

1. Preheat the oven to 350°F. Brush two 8-inch round cake pans with the melted butter and line the bottom of each with parchment paper.

2. Using a hand mixer or a stand mixer fitted with the paddle attachment, beat the softened butter and granulated sugar on medium speed until fluffy and light. Beat the eggs in one at a time, then beat in the vanilla and orange zest.

3. In a small bowl, whisk together the flour, baking powder, and salt. Fold the flour mixture into the butter mixture just until combined. Divide the batter between the cake pans.

4. Bake for 20 to 25 minutes or until the cakes are golden and a toothpick inserted in the middle of the cake comes out clean. Let the cakes cool in the pans for 5 minutes, then turn out onto a wire rack, remove the parchment, and let cool completely.

5. Lightly whip the cream with a whisk until stiff peaks form. Set aside. Place 1 cake layer on a serving plate, spread the raspberry jam evenly on the cake, and top with the whipped cream. Sprinkle the raspberries over the whipped cream, reserving some for decoration. Place the other cake layer on top and dust with the confectioners' sugar. Arrange the reserved raspberries in the center of the cake. Slice and serve.

Old-Fashioned Fruitcake

Yield: Serves 8 to 10 | Prep Time: 30 minutes | Cook Time: 1½ to 2 hours

Fruitcake is a time-honored classic that was first popularized back in the sixteenth century when it was discovered that fruit could be preserved for long periods of time if baked into a sugary fruitcake. While refrigerators help render that purpose unnecessary today, fruitcake can still be a delicious dessert, especially when you can liven it up with a touch of brandy, like I do here.

INGREDIENTS

½ cup chopped dried apricots

½ cup dried cranberries

½ cup dried cherries

¼ cup golden raisins

¼ cup dried currants

¼ cup chopped dried pineapple

1 cup brandy

½ cup chopped pistachios

½ cup chopped hazelnuts, raw

½ cup chopped pecans

½ cup sliced almonds

12 tablespoons (1½ sticks) unsalted butter, softened

1 cup packed light brown sugar

2 large eggs

2 tablespoons grated orange zest

2 teaspoons vanilla bean paste or vanilla extract

¼ teaspoon ground cinnamon

¼ teaspoon ground nutmeg

2 pinches kosher salt

1½ cups all-purpose flour

1 teaspoon baking powder

Turbinado sugar for sprinkling

DIRECTIONS

1. Preheat the oven to 350°F. Grease a 9 × 5-inch loaf pan.

2. In a medium bowl, combine the apricots, cranberries, cherries, raisins, currants, and pineapple. In a small saucepan, heat the brandy to a simmer, about 5 minutes. Pour over the fruit and let it macerate for 10 minutes. Drain the fruit and reserve the brandy. Place the fruit in another bowl and mix with the pistachios, hazelnuts, pecans, and almonds.

3. Using a hand mixer or a stand mixer fitted with the whisk attachment, cream the butter on medium speed for a minute, then add the brown sugar and mix until fluffy, about 5 minutes. Add the eggs, one at a time, beating until combined. Scrape down the bowl, then beat in the orange zest, vanilla, cinnamon, nutmeg, and salt. On low speed, beat in the flour and baking powder.

4. Fold the fruit and nut mixture into the batter. Pour the batter into the loaf pan and smooth the top. Sprinkle turbinado sugar over the top.

5. Bake for 1½ to 2 hours or until the cake is golden and a toothpick inserted in the center comes out clean.

6. While the cake is baking, bring the reserved brandy back to a simmer and reduce by half. When the cake comes out of the oven, pour the brandy over the cake. Let the cake cool fully in the pan before slicing and serving.

Refrigerator Fudge Cake

Yield: Serves 12 | Prep Time: 15 minutes, plus 6 hours chill time | Cook Time: 10 to 15 minutes

My nephew begged me to make him a special ice cream cake for his 4th birthday, and when I brought him this, he was ecstatic. The adults at the party loved it too, since the cream cheese layer gives it a cheesecake-like sophistication.

INGREDIENTS

1½ cups all-purpose flour

1 cup chopped pecans

12 tablespoons (1½ sticks) unsalted butter, melted

3 cups milk, cold

2 (3.4-ounce) boxes chocolate instant pudding mix

1 teaspoon espresso powder

12 ounces cream cheese, room temperature

1 cup confectioners' sugar

1 (16-ounce) container frozen whipped topping, thawed

Chopped bittersweet dark chocolate for decorating

DIRECTIONS

1. Preheat the oven to 350°F. Lightly grease a 9 × 13-inch baking dish.

2. In a medium bowl, mix the flour, ¾ cup of the pecans, and the melted butter. Evenly press the mixture into the baking dish. Bake for 10 to 15 minutes or until the crust is firm. Let cool.

3. In a medium bowl, whisk together the milk, pudding mix, and espresso powder for 2 minutes. Let sit for 5 minutes until thickened. In another medium bowl, mix the cream cheese, confectioners' sugar, and half of the whipped topping until combined.

4. Spread the cream cheese mixture over the cooled crust. Evenly spread the chocolate pudding over the cream cheese mixture. Top with the remaining whipped topping.

5. Sprinkle the remaining pecans and some chopped chocolate over the top.

6. Refrigerate for 6 hours. Slice and serve.

Lemon Shortcake Icebox Cake

Yield: Serves 12 | Prep Time: 25 minutes | Chill Time: 4 to 6 hours

You get the best of both worlds from the ladyfingers. They look elegant, but since they're already made, they're super easy to add to any dessert. The light lemon touch makes this dessert ideal for a cool spring day.

INGREDIENTS

2 cups heavy cream

1¾ cups confectioners' sugar

1 (8-ounce) container mascarpone cheese, room temperature

2 cups lemon curd (homemade or jarred)

1 tablespoon grated lemon zest

2 cups milk

2 teaspoons vanilla bean paste or vanilla extract

2 (7-ounce) packages dry savoiardi ladyfingers

Fresh raspberries for serving

DIRECTIONS

1. Using a hand mixer or a stand mixer with a chilled bowl and whisk attachment, beat the cream on medium-high speed. Slowly add 1¼ cups of the confectioners' sugar and beat until stiff peaks form. Transfer to a bowl and refrigerate.

2. If using a stand mixer, switch to the paddle attachment. Put the mascarpone cheese in the mixer bowl and beat on medium-high speed until light and fluffy. Reduce the speed to low and beat in the lemon curd and lemon zest until combined. Slowly beat in the remaining ½ cup confectioners' sugar until completely incorporated, scraping down the bowl as needed. Fold 2 cups of the whipped cream into the lemon-mascarpone mixture.

3. Line a 9-inch square baking dish with parchment paper.

4. In a small bowl, combine the milk and vanilla. Working with one at a time, dip the ladyfingers in the milk mixture and line the bottom of the baking dish with them, cutting to fit if necessary. Spread half of the lemon-mascarpone filling over the ladyfingers. Repeat with another layer of ladyfingers, then the remaining lemon-mascarpone filling. Smooth the top. Spread the remaining whipped cream over the filling.

5. Cover and refrigerate for 4 to 6 hours until the layers are set.

6. Sprinkle with fresh raspberries. Slice and serve.

No-Bake Strawberry Icebox Cake

Yield: Serves 8 | Prep Time: 15 minutes | Chill Time: 4 to 5 hours

Strawberries might just be my favorite fruit to make desserts with. Not only are they universally loved, thereby pleasing all of my guests, but their bright red coloring makes any dessert that features them a real standout.

INGREDIENTS

1 (8-ounce) container mascarpone cheese, room temperature

1 (8-ounce) container frozen whipped topping, thawed

1 cup milk

½ teaspoon vanilla bean paste or vanilla extract

2 (7-ounce) packages dry savoiardi ladyfingers

2 pounds fresh strawberries, sliced, some whole strawberries reserved (optional)

2 ounces bittersweet dark chocolate, chopped

1 teaspoon coconut oil

DIRECTIONS

1. Line a 9-inch square baking dish with parchment paper.

2. In a medium bowl, combine the mascarpone cheese with the whipped topping.

3. In a small bowl, combine the milk and vanilla. Working with one at a time, dip the ladyfingers in the milk mixture and line the bottom of the baking dish with them, cutting to fit if necessary. Top the ladyfingers with half of the mascarpone mixture, then add a layer of sliced strawberries. Repeat with another layer of the ladyfingers, the remaining mascarpone mixture, then a layer of strawberries, sliced, whole, or both.

4. Combine the chopped chocolate and coconut oil in a small microwave-safe bowl and microwave on high in 15-second intervals or until melted. Drizzle over the top of the cake.

5. Refrigerate for 4–5 hours. Slice and serve.

Pistachio Icebox Cake

Yield: Serves 9 | Prep Time: 10 to 15 minutes | Chill Time: 8 hours

Pistachios are an underrated ingredient for desserts. In this light summertime dessert, the soft green color of the pistachios looks gorgeous against the white topping. With only five ingredients, this cake is not only elegant, but easy to create.

INGREDIENTS

2¼ cups milk

2 (3.4-ounce) boxes pistachio instant pudding mix

1 (8-ounce) container frozen whipped topping, thawed

2 (10-ounce) boxes Lorna Doone shortbread cookies (55 cookies)

1 cup chopped pistachios for decorating

DIRECTIONS

1. Line an 8-inch square baking dish with parchment paper.

2. In a large bowl, whisk the milk and pudding mix until thickened and smooth. Refrigerate for 5 minutes.

3. Reserve 1 cup of the whipped topping and fold the remaining topping into the pudding.

4. Layer 25 shortbread cookies in the bottom of the baking dish. Top with half of the pudding–whipped topping mixture. Repeat the layers. Top with the reserved whipped topping. Refrigerate for 8 hours. Crush the remaining 5 cookies and sprinkle over the whipped topping. Top with the chopped pistachios. Slice and serve.

4

Everyday Cakes

When it comes to cake, I don't need to wait for a holiday or birthday to enjoy a slice of my favorite. It's so easy to bake a cake like Texas Tornado Cake (page 92) or Mint Patty Cake (page 112) on a Sunday and enjoy slices after dinner and throughout the rest of the week. And with my husband's penchant for sweets, he's certainly not complaining.

Classic Texas Sheet Cake

Yield: Serves 24 to 28 | Prep Time: 25 minutes | Cook Time: 25 to 30 minutes

The exact origins of Texas sheet cake remain a mystery. While versions of this recipe have been around since the early 1900s, the use of sour cream instead of buttermilk was a newer adaptation adopted in the 1970s when sour cream was becoming a trendier ingredient. It's a dessert that still finds a purpose today because it's easy to serve to a large crowd.

INGREDIENTS

Cake

16 tablespoons (2 sticks) unsalted butter

¼ cup cocoa powder

½ teaspoon espresso powder

2 cups all-purpose flour

2 cups granulated sugar

2 large eggs

½ cup sour cream

1 teaspoon baking soda

½ teaspoon kosher salt

Frosting

4 tablespoons unsalted butter

6 tablespoons heavy cream

2 tablespoons cocoa powder

¼ teaspoon espresso powder

3½ cups confectioners' sugar

1 teaspoon vanilla bean paste or vanilla extract

¾ cup chopped pecans

DIRECTIONS

1. Preheat the oven to 350°F. Lightly grease a 10 × 15-inch jelly-roll pan.

2. *For the cake:* In a small saucepan, combine the butter, cocoa powder, espresso powder, and 1 cup water. Cook over low heat until the butter is melted. Remove from the heat and pour into a large bowl to cool, about 3 minutes. Whisk in the flour, granulated sugar, eggs, sour cream, baking soda, and salt.

3. Pour the batter into the pan. Bake for 25 minutes or until the cake is set and a toothpick inserted in the center comes out clean. Let the cake cool in the pan.

4. *For the frosting:* In a small saucepan, melt the butter, cream, cocoa powder, and espresso powder over low heat. Remove from the heat and transfer to a large bowl. Slowly beat in confectioners' sugar and vanilla until creamy and smooth. Spread the frosting over the cooled cake. Sprinkle the top with chopped pecans. Slice and serve.

Amish Applesauce Cake

Yield: Serves 12 | Prep Time: 15 minutes | Cook Time: 30 to 35 minutes

Applesauce is an ideal addition to many cake batters because it helps keep the cake moist. The use of vegetable shortening instead of butter affects the texture of the cake, making it tender, lofty, and light.

INGREDIENTS

1 cup sugar

½ cup vegetable shortening

2 large eggs

2 cups all-purpose flour

½ teaspoon ground cinnamon

½ teaspoon ground cardamom

1 teaspoon baking soda

½ teaspoon kosher salt

1½ cups applesauce

1 apple, peeled, cored, and diced

½ cup pecans

1 teaspoon vanilla bean paste or vanilla extract

Caramel sauce for drizzling

DIRECTIONS

1. Preheat the oven to 350°F. Grease a 9 × 13-inch baking dish.

2. Using a hand mixer or a stand mixer fitted with the paddle attachment, beat the sugar and shortening on low speed until fluffy. Add the eggs, one at a time, beating until incorporated. Add the flour, cinnamon, cardamom, baking soda, and salt. Beat until well combined. Fold in the applesauce, apple, pecans, and vanilla.

3. Pour the batter into the baking dish and bake for 30 to 35 minutes or until the cake is golden and a toothpick inserted in the center comes out clean.

4. Let the cake cool in the pan, then slice and serve with a drizzle of caramel sauce.

Grandma's Magic Cake

Yield: Serves 8 | Prep Time: 15 to 20 minutes plus 3 hours chill time | Cook Time: 1 hour

The magic cake is aptly named because although the batter is poured into the baking dish all at once, while it cooks, it separates into three distinct layers—a dense bottom layer, a custardy middle layer, and a fluffy, cakey top layer. This magic separation of layers is due to a couple of factors. The large quantity of liquid helps create a dense base and the lower oven temperature allows the batter more time to settle. This cake takes a long time to cool, so make sure to allow enough time for that before serving.

INGREDIENTS

¾ cup all-purpose flour, plus extra for the pan

4 large eggs, separated, room temperature

½ teaspoon lemon juice

½ cup plus 2 tablespoons granulated sugar

2 teaspoons vanilla bean paste or vanilla extract

8 tablespoons (1 stick) plus 2 teaspoons unsalted butter, melted

⅛ teaspoon kosher salt

2 cups milk, lukewarm

Confectioners' sugar, for dusting

DIRECTIONS

1. Preheat the oven to 325°F. Grease and flour an 8-inch square baking dish.

2. Using a hand mixer or a stand mixer fitted with the whisk attachment, whip the egg whites with the lemon juice until stiff peaks form. Transfer to another bowl.

3. If using a stand mixer, switch to the paddle attachment. Put the egg yolks, granulated sugar, vanilla, and 1 tablespoon water in the mixer bowl and beat on medium speed until smooth. Add the melted butter and beat for 1 minute. On low speed, beat in in the flour and salt. Add the milk and beat until fully combined.

4. Carefully fold in the egg whites. Do not over-incorporate; there should be some clouds of egg whites in the batter.

5. Pour the batter into the baking dish and bake for 1 hour or until the top is golden and softly set. Check at the halfway point and cover with foil if the top is browning too quickly.

6. Let the cake cool in the baking dish for 3 hours. Dust with confectioners' sugar. Slice and serve.

Lemon Poppy Seed Cake

Yield: Serves 8 to 10 | Prep Time: 15 minutes | Cook Time: 30 minutes

When the dark, cold days start to creep up on me, I like to make something light and lemony, like this lemon poppy seed cake, to brighten my spirits.

INGREDIENTS

Cake

1¼ cups all-purpose flour

1 teaspoon baking powder

1 teaspoon grated lemon zest

¼ teaspoon salt

16 tablespoons (2 sticks) unsalted butter, softened

¾ cup granulated sugar

2 large eggs

2 tablespoons poppy seeds

Glaze

1½ cups confectioners' sugar

3 tablespoons lemon juice

Orange zest

DIRECTIONS

1. Preheat the oven to 375°F. Grease a 9-inch springform pan.

2. *For the cake:* In a large bowl, whisk together the flour, baking powder, lemon zest, and salt.

3. Using a hand mixer or a stand mixer fitted with the paddle attachment, beat the butter and granulated sugar at medium speed 2 to 3 minutes or until pale and fluffy. Beat in the eggs until combined. Reduce the speed to low, then add the flour mixture and poppy seeds and mix until just combined.

4. Pour the batter into the cake pan and smooth the top. Bake for 30 minutes until the cake is golden and a toothpick inserted in the center comes out clean. Let the cake cool in the pan for 5 minutes, then turn out onto a wire rack to cool completely. Move to a serving plate.

5. *For the glaze:* In a small bowl, whisk together the confectioners' sugar and lemon juice until smooth. Pour the glaze over the warm cake, spreading it with a spatula to drizzle over the edge. Let it stand until the glaze is set, about 15 minutes.

6. Top with orange zest. Slice and serve.

Church Cake

Yield: Serves 12 to 16 │ Prep Time: 25 minutes │ Cook Time: 40 to 50 minutes

Often, when my husband and I attend church, there will be a snack table in the back where attendees can grab cookies, pastries, and other treats on their way home. I like to contribute a cake such as this one, since it has enough flavorful elements to be interesting without requiring as much finesse as a layer cake. Baking it in a casserole dish also makes it super-portable.

INGREDIENTS

Cake

3 cups all-purpose flour

2 teaspoons baking soda

1 teaspoon kosher salt

½ teaspoon ground cinnamon

¼ teaspoon ground nutmeg

2 cups granulated sugar

3 large eggs

1 cup vegetable or canola oil

2 teaspoons rum extract

1 (20-ounce) can crushed pineapple with juice

1½ cups finely chopped walnuts

1 cup sweetened shredded coconut

Frosting

8 ounces cream cheese, room temperature

8 tablespoons (1 stick) unsalted butter, softened

1 teaspoon vanilla bean paste or vanilla extract

2 cups confectioners' sugar

DIRECTIONS

1. Preheat the oven to 350°F. Grease a 9 × 13-inch baking dish.

2. *For the cake:* In a medium bowl, whisk together the flour, baking soda, salt, cinnamon, and nutmeg.

3. Using a hand mixer or a stand mixer fitted with the paddle attachment, beat the sugar, eggs, oil, and rum extract on medium speed until fluffy. On low speed, gradually add the flour mixture and beat until combined. Add the pineapple, 1 cup of the chopped walnuts, and the coconut. Beat just until combined.

4. Pour the cake batter into the baking dish and bake for 40 to 50 minutes until the cake is golden and a toothpick inserted in the center comes out clean. Let cool in the pan.

5. *For the frosting:* Using a hand mixer or a stand mixer fitted with the paddle attachment, beat the cream cheese, butter, and vanilla until light and fluffy. Gradually beat in the confectioners' sugar until smooth and spreadable. Frost the top of the cake and sprinkle the remaining ½ cup walnuts over the frosting. Slice and serve.

Best-Ever German Chocolate Cake

Yield: Serves 12 | Prep Time: 20 minutes plus 30 minutes cooling time | Cook Time: 30 to 35 minutes

A German chocolate cake tends to include a bit more sugar than a regular chocolate cake, making it even sweeter (and in my opinion, more delectable).

INGREDIENTS

Cake

2 cups all-purpose flour, plus extra for the pans

2 cups sugar

¾ cup cocoa powder

2 teaspoons baking powder

1½ teaspoons baking soda

1 teaspoon kosher salt

1 cup milk

½ cup vegetable or canola oil

2 large eggs

2 teaspoons vanilla bean paste or vanilla extract

1 cup boiling water

Frosting

1 cup evaporated milk

1 tablespoon cornstarch

1 cup sugar

3 large egg yolks mixed with 1 teaspoon water

8 tablespoons (1 stick) unsalted butter, cut into small pieces

1 teaspoon vanilla bean paste or vanilla extract

1 cup chopped pecans

1 cup sweetened flaked coconut

Chocolate Drizzle

2 ounces bittersweet dark chocolate, chopped

1 teaspoon coconut oil

DIRECTIONS

1. Preheat the oven to 350°F. Line two 9-inch round cake pans with parchment paper. Grease and flour the parchment.

2. *For the cake:* Using a hand mixer or a stand mixer fitted with the paddle attachment, blend the flour, sugar, cocoa, baking powder, baking soda, and salt on medium speed. Add the milk, vegetable oil, eggs, and vanilla and beat until combined. Reduce the speed to low and carefully add the boiling water, a bit at a time, until mixed in. Beat on high speed for 1 minute.

3. Divide the cake batter between the cake pans and bake for 30 to 35 minutes or until set and a toothpick comes out clean.

4. Let the cakes cool in the pans for 10 minutes, then turn out onto a wire rack, remove the parchment, and let cool completely.

5. *For the frosting:* In a large saucepan, combine the evaporated milk and cornstarch, mixing until well combined. Stir in the sugar, egg yolk mixture, butter, and vanilla. Cook over medium-low heat until the mixture begins to boil. Stir the mixture constantly for about 10 minutes until thickened. Remove from the heat and stir in the pecans and coconut. Let the frosting cool for about an hour.

6. Place a cake layer on a serving plate and spread half of the frosting over the cake. Add the second layer and spread with the remaining half of the frosting.

7. *For the chocolate drizzle:* Place the chopped chocolate and coconut oil in a bowl and microwave until the chocolate is melted. Stir until smooth. Drizzle over the cake. Slice and serve.

Texas Tornado Cake

Yield: Serves 16 | Prep Time: 15 minutes | Cook Time: 40 to 45 minutes

This dessert is based on a popular dessert served at Duff's Famous Smorgasbord in Tennessee back in the 1980s and '90s. It contains such a whirlwind concoction of ingredients that it's almost as if a tornado had blown right through the kitchen.

INGREDIENTS

Cake

2 cups all-purpose flour, plus extra for the pan

1½ cups granulated sugar

1 (16-ounce) can fruit cocktail with syrup

2 large eggs

2 teaspoons baking soda

1 teaspoon rum extract

1 cup chopped pecans

¼ cup packed light brown sugar

Icing

1 cup sweetened shredded coconut

8 tablespoons (1 stick) unsalted butter

¾ cup packed light brown sugar

½ cup heavy cream

1 teaspoon coconut extract

DIRECTIONS

1. Preheat the oven to 325°F. Grease and flour a 9 × 13-inch baking dish.

2. *For the cake:* In a large bowl, stir the flour, sugar, fruit cocktail, eggs, baking soda, and rum extract until combined. Pour into the baking dish. In a small bowl, mix the pecans and brown sugar. Sprinkle over the cake.

3. Bake for 40 to 45 minutes or until the cake is golden and a toothpick inserted in the center comes out clean. Transfer the pan to a wire rack.

4. *For the icing:* After the cake is cool, in a small saucepan, combine the coconut, butter, brown sugar, cream, and coconut extract. Bring to a boil over medium heat and cook for 2 minutes, being careful not to let it burn. Spoon the icing over the hot cake. Let the cake cool before slicing and serving.

Inside-Out Cream Puff Cake

Yield: Serves 8 to 10 | Prep Time: 25 minutes | Cook Time: 30 minutes

This cake is light as air! The soft, cushiony crust acts as a platform for the sweet whipped topping center. It's amazing how similar it is to those handheld cream puffs you may pick up at the local bakery—there's just so much more to enjoy here.

INGREDIENTS

Cream Puff Crust

8 tablespoons (1 stick) unsalted butter

1 cup all-purpose flour

4 large eggs

Filling

8 ounces cream cheese, room temperature

1 (5.1-ounce) box vanilla instant pudding mix

3 cups milk

1½ cups heavy cream

2–3 tablespoons confectioners' sugar

1 teaspoon vanilla bean paste or vanilla extract

½ cup bittersweet chocolate chips

1 teaspoon coconut oil

DIRECTIONS

1. Preheat the oven to 400°F. Grease a 9 × 13-inch baking dish.

2. *For the cream puff crust:* In a medium saucepan, bring the butter and 1 cup water to a boil. Whisk in the flour and take off the heat. Let the mixture cool for a few minutes. With a wooden spoon, stir in the eggs, one at a time, until fully incorporated.

3. Spread the mixture evenly into the baking dish. Bake for 30 minutes. The crust will puff up around the edges. Let the crust cool completely in the pan.

4. *For the filling:* Using a hand mixer or a stand mixer fitted with the paddle attachment, beat the cream cheese on medium speed for 1 to 2 minutes until light and fluffy. Beat in the pudding mix, then slowly add the milk. Blend until smooth. Fill the cream puff crust with the cream cheese mixture.

5. With a clean mixer, whip the cream, confectioners' sugar, and vanilla until medium-stiff peaks form. Spread over the cream cheese mixture.

6. Melt the chocolate chips with the coconut oil in the microwave. Drizzle over the whipped cream. Slice and serve.

Cinnamon Roll Cake Roll

Yield: Serves 8 to 10 | Prep Time: 25 minutes plus 30 minutes cooling time | Cook Time: 7 to 9 minutes

This cake roll has everything you love from the classic breakfast pastry with its combination of cinnamon and cream cheese.

INGREDIENTS

Cake Roll

3 large eggs

¾ cup granulated sugar

1 teaspoon vanilla bean paste or vanilla extract

1 cup plus 2 tablespoons all-purpose flour

1 teaspoon baking powder

⅛ teaspoon kosher salt

5 tablespoons unsalted butter

⅓ cup packed light brown sugar

1½ teaspoons ground cinnamon

¼ teaspoon ground nutmeg

Filling

8 ounces cream cheese, room temperature

½ cup confectioners' sugar

1 teaspoon ground cinnamon

1 cup frozen whipped topping, thawed

Glaze

3 tablespoons heavy cream

1 teaspoon vanilla bean paste or vanilla extract

1½ cups confectioners' sugar

DIRECTIONS

1. Preheat the oven to 375°F. Lightly coat an 11 × 17-inch rimmed baking pan with cooking spray. Line with parchment paper, leaving a small overhang on the short sides. Spray with cooking spray.

2. *For the cake roll:* Beat the eggs on medium for about 5 minutes until thickened. Gradually beat in the granulated sugar. Reduce to low and beat in the vanilla and ⅓ cup water. Slowly add 1 cup of the flour, the baking powder, and salt and mix. Pour into the baking pan.

3. In a small saucepan, melt the butter. Stir in the brown sugar, cinnamon, nutmeg, and the remaining 2 tablespoons flour until smooth and blended. Drizzle over the cake batter and swirl in.

4. Bake for 7 to 9 minutes or until set. Let cool in the pan for 5 minutes. Lift the cake out and place it on a flat surface. Using the parchment paper, roll up the cake starting at the short end. Place on a wire rack and let cool for about 30 minutes.

5. *For the filling:* Beat the cream cheese on medium until smooth. Reduce to low and beat in the confectioners' sugar and cinnamon. Increase the speed to medium-high and beat until the filling is light. Reduce to low and fold in the whipped topping until combined.

6. Carefully unroll the cake. Spread the filling over the cake, leaving a 1-inch border on the short ends. Carefully reroll the cake, peeling the parchment as you go. Place the cake on a serving platter.

7. *For the glaze:* Heat the cream and vanilla until warm. Whisk in the confectioners' sugar. Drizzle over the cake roll. Slice and serve.

Almond Honey Cake

Yield: Serves 12 | Prep Time: 20 minutes | Cook Time: 1 hour 10 minutes to 1 hour 25 minutes

This is one of my favorite types of cake to eat on a spring afternoon with a cool glass of lemonade on the side. The best part about this is that it's made with almond flour instead of wheat flour, so your gluten-free friends can feel free to indulge as well!

INGREDIENTS

¼ cup olive oil, plus extra for the pan

2 cups almond flour, plus extra for the pan

½ teaspoon kosher salt

1½ cups sugar

⅔ cup honey

2 tablespoons lemon zest

4 large eggs, separated, plus 2 large egg whites

½ teaspoon vanilla bean paste or vanilla extract

¼ teaspoon almond extract

3 tablespoons lemon juice

Assorted fresh berries for decorating

DIRECTIONS

1. Preheat the oven to 325°F. Brush the bottom and sides of a 9-inch springform pan with oil. Line the bottom with parchment paper. Brush the parchment paper with a bit of oil and sprinkle almond flour over the bottom and sides of the pan.

2. Combine the almond flour and salt in a small bowl.

3. Using a hand mixer or a stand mixer fitted with the paddle attachment, beat ½ cup of the sugar, ⅓ cup of the honey, the lemon zest, egg yolks, vanilla, almond extract, and oil on medium speed until smooth and creamy. Beat in the almond flour mixture until incorporated. Transfer to another large bowl.

4. Using a hand mixer or a stand mixer fitted with the whisk attachment, whip the egg whites until frothy. Slowly add ½ cup sugar and beat 3 to 4 minutes or until glossy peaks form. Gently fold the egg whites into the cake batter.

5. Pour into the pan. Bake for 50 to 55 minutes, until the cake is golden and a toothpick inserted in the center comes out clean. Let the cake cool completely in the pan, then remove the ring.

6. In a small saucepan, combine the remaining ½ cup sugar, the remaining ⅓ cup honey, the lemon juice, and 1 cup water. Bring the mixture to a simmer over high heat. Reduce to medium heat and simmer for 20 to 30 minutes or until thick.

7. Brush some of the syrup over the cake. Top the cake with berries, then drizzle more syrup over the berries. Slice and serve.

Zucchini Cake with Browned Butter Frosting

Yield: Serves 9 to 12 | Prep Time: 20 minutes | Cook Time: 40 to 45 minutes

The extra moisture from the zucchini makes this cake denser than ordinary white cakes, which makes it an intriguing option on a hot and stuffy summer day.

INGREDIENTS

Cake

1 cup all-purpose flour

1 teaspoon ground cinnamon

1 teaspoon baking soda

½ teaspoon kosher salt

¼ teaspoon ground nutmeg

⅛ teaspoon baking powder

2 large eggs

1 cup granulated sugar

½ cup vegetable oil

1 tablespoon vanilla bean paste or vanilla extract

1 zucchini, shredded and drained (about 1 cup)

½ cup chopped pecans

Frosting

3 tablespoons unsalted butter

2 cups confectioners' sugar

1–2 tablespoons heavy cream

DIRECTIONS

1. *For the cake:* Preheat the oven to 350°F. Grease a 9-inch square baking dish. Line the dish with parchment paper, leaving an overhang on 2 sides.

2. In a small bowl, whisk the flour, cinnamon, baking soda, salt, nutmeg, and baking powder.

3. In a large bowl, beat the eggs, then beat in the granulated sugar until combined. Stir in the oil and vanilla. Add the flour mixture and stir until incorporated. Fold in the zucchini and pecans. Spread into the baking dish.

4. Bake for 40 to 45 minutes or until the cake is browned and a toothpick inserted in the center comes out clean. Let the cake cool for 10 minutes in the pan. Then use the parchment paper to transfer to a serving plate.

5. *For the frosting:* In a small saucepan, melt the butter over medium-low heat and let it cook until it starts to sizzle and brown. Watch it carefully and do not let it burn. Remove from the heat, let it cool slightly, and then transfer to a small bowl. Whisk in the confectioners' sugar and gradually add the cream until you have a spreadable consistency. Frost the cake. Slice and serve.

Millionaire Marshmallow Fluff Cake

Yield: Serves 12 | Prep Time: 25 minutes plus 4 hours chill time | Cook Time: 5 to 7 minutes

The light-as-air center combined with the rich taste of toasted coconut makes you feel like a million bucks. This cake is especially fitting for a warm summer day when you need the perfect dessert to help you cool down.

INGREDIENTS

1 cup plus 3 tablespoons graham cracker crumbs

¼ cup sugar

4 tablespoons unsalted butter, melted

⅓ cup milk

20 marshmallows

8 ounces cream cheese, room temperature

½ teaspoon vanilla bean paste or vanilla extract

1 (8-ounce) container frozen whipped topping, thawed

½ teaspoon ground cinnamon

¼ cup sweetened shredded coconut, toasted

DIRECTIONS

1. Preheat the oven to 350°F. Lightly grease an 8-inch square baking dish.

2. In a small bowl, combine 1 cup of the graham cracker crumbs, the sugar, and melted butter. Press evenly into the baking dish. Bake for 5 to 7 minutes or until set. Set aside to cool.

3. In a small saucepan, combine the milk and marshmallows. Cook on low heat until the marshmallows have melted. Set aside. Using a hand mixer or a stand mixer fitted with the paddle attachment, beat the cream cheese and vanilla on medium speed until light and fluffy. Add the marshmallow mixture and beat until combined. Fold in the whipped topping. Pour the filling into the baking dish.

4. Combine the remaining 3 tablespoons graham cracker crumbs with the cinnamon. Sprinkle over the cake, then sprinkle the toasted coconut over the top. Refrigerate for at least 4 hours until firm. Slice and serve.

NOTES

To toast the coconut, spread it on a baking sheet and bake at 350°F for 5 to 10 minutes or until light golden brown.

Moist, Fluffy Coconut Cake

Yield: Serves 16 | Prep Time: 45 minutes plus 2 hours chill time | Cook Time: 25 to 30 minutes

I've always been a big fan of coconut cake. The blanket of snowy coconut makes it look much fancier and more sophisticated than it is.

INGREDIENTS

Cake

2½ cups cake flour

1 teaspoon baking soda

1 teaspoon kosher salt

¾ cup buttermilk

¼ cup coconut milk

1½ teaspoons vanilla bean paste or vanilla extract

1 teaspoon coconut extract

½ teaspoon almond extract

16 tablespoons (2 sticks) unsalted butter, softened

2 cups granulated sugar

5 large eggs

Cream Cheese Frosting

12 ounces cream cheese, room temperature

10 tablespoons plus 2 teaspoons unsalted butter, softened

4⅓ cups confectioners' sugar

1¼ teaspoons coconut extract

2 cups sweetened shredded coconut

DIRECTIONS

1. Preheat the oven to 350°F. Grease three 9-inch round cake pans. Line the pans with parchment paper.

2. *For the cake:* In a medium bowl, whisk together the flour, baking soda, and salt. In a small bowl, mix the buttermilk, coconut milk, vanilla, coconut extract, and almond extract.

3. Using a hand mixer or a stand mixer fitted with the paddle attachment, beat the butter on medium speed for 1 minute. Gradually add the granulated sugar and beat for about 3 minutes until light and fluffy. Add the eggs one at a time, beating until incorporated.

4. On low speed, add the flour mixture to the butter mixture in 3 batches, alternating with the buttermilk mixture in 2 batches; beat.

5. Divide the batter between the cake pans. Bake for 25 to 30 minutes or until the cake is golden and a toothpick inserted in the center comes out clean. Let the cakes cool in the pans for 15 minutes, then turn out onto a wire rack, remove the parchment, and let cool completely.

6. *For the cream cheese frosting:* Using a hand mixer or a stand mixer fitted with the paddle attachment, beat the cream cheese with the butter on medium speed until fluffy. Add the confectioners' sugar and coconut extract and beat until smooth and spreadable.

7. Place 1 cake layer on a serving plate, spread ½ cup frosting evenly over the cake, then sprinkle one-third of the coconut over the frosting. Repeat, then top with the third cake layer. Spread the remaining frosting over the top and sides of the cake. Carefully sprinkle and lightly press the remaining coconut over the top and sides of the cake. Refrigerate for 2 hours before slicing and serving.

Blueberry Angel Food Sheet Cake

Yield: Serves 24 to 30 | Prep Time: 10 minutes | Cook Time: 25 to 30 minutes

This cake boasts the soft fluffiness that's the signature of an angel food cake, but since it's made in a sheet pan, it's easier to serve to a crowd.

INGREDIENTS

Cake

1 (16-ounce) box angel food cake mix

Vegetable oil as needed for the cake mix

Eggs as needed for the cake mix

1 cup fresh or thawed frozen blueberries

1 teaspoon all-purpose flour

Glaze

1 cup fresh or thawed frozen blueberries

1 tablespoon granulated sugar

2 teaspoons grated lemon zest plus 1 tablespoon lemon juice

2 cups confectioners' sugar

½ teaspoon vanilla bean paste or vanilla extract

DIRECTIONS

1. *For the cake:* Preheat the oven and prepare the angel food cake batter according to the package directions. Pour the batter into an ungreased 12 × 18-inch rimmed baking sheet.

2. In a small bowl, combine the blueberries and flour, then sprinkle the blueberries evenly over the batter. Bake for 25 to 30 minutes or until the cake is lightly golden. Let the cake cool in the pan.

3. *For the glaze:* Combine the blueberries, granulated sugar, lemon zest and juice, and 2 tablespoons water in a small saucepan. Heat to a simmer and cook for 2 minutes. In a medium bowl, whisk the blueberry mixture with the confectioners' sugar and vanilla until smooth. Pour the glaze over the cake. Slice and serve.

Heaven and Hell Cake

Yield: Serves 8 to 10 | Prep Time: 20 minutes plus 2 hours chill time | Cook Time: 1 hour 20 minutes

When the angel on your shoulder tells you to make one cake and the devil points to another, it doesn't hurt to listen to both! This cake is the epitome of compromise: half rich devil's food cake and half smooth, airy angel food cake with a creamy peanut butter mousse in between.

INGREDIENTS

Ganache

1 cup heavy cream

2 cups semisweet chocolate chips

Cakes

1 (16-ounce) box angel food cake mix

1 (15.25-ounce) box devil's food cake mix

Vegetable oil as needed for the cake mix

Eggs as needed for the cake mix

Peanut Butter Mousse

1 cup heavy cream

1 pound cream cheese, room temperature

3 cups smooth peanut butter, room temperature

2 cups confectioners' sugar

DIRECTIONS

1. Preheat the oven to 350°F.

2. *For the ganache:* Heat the cream just until simmering. Place the chocolate chips in a heatproof bowl, pour the hot cream over them, and let stand for 2 to 3 minutes, then stir until smooth. Cover with plastic wrap and set aside at room temperature until you are ready to frost.

3. *For the cakes:* Make the angel food cake according to the package directions, using two ungreased 9-inch round cake pans. Bake for 45 to 50 minutes or until the top springs back when touched. Transfer the pans to a wire rack and let cool completely. Make the devil's food cake according to the package directions, using two ungreased 9-inch round cake pans. Transfer to a wire rack and let cool completely.

4. *For the peanut butter mousse:* Using a hand mixer or a stand mixer fitted with the paddle attachment, whip the cream on medium-high speed for 2 to 3 minutes or until stiff peaks form. Transfer the cream to a separate bowl. Add the cream cheese, peanut butter, and confectioners' sugar on medium speed for 3 minutes or until fluffy. Using a spatula, fold one-third of the whipped cream into the peanut butter mixture, then fold in the remaining two-thirds. Cover and refrigerate until ready to use.

5. *To assemble:* Place 1 devil's food cake layer on a serving plate and spread one-third of the peanut butter mousse over the top. Top the mousse with an angel food cake layer and spread with half of the remaining mousse. Repeat with the remaining devil's food cake layer, mousse, and angel food cake layer.

6. Stir the ganache. Frost the top and sides of the cake with the ganache. Refrigerate the cake for 2 hours before slicing and serving.

NOTES

If you have enough cake pans, you can bake the angel food cake and devil's food cake at the same time.

Italian Love Cake

Yield: Serves 12 | Prep Time: 15 minutes plus 6 hours chill time | Cook Time: 55 minutes to 1 hour

Nothing says "love" like this triple-textured chocolate cake. The coolest part about this recipe is how the ricotta cheese mixture and box cake mixture switch places in the middle of baking! The density of the ricotta cheese weighs that layer down, allowing it to sink to the bottom, but not before the cake mix layer leaves behind a thin bottom crust. How neat is that?

INGREDIENTS

Cake

1 (15.25-ounce) box chocolate cake mix

Vegetable oil as needed for the cake mix

4 large eggs, plus eggs as needed for the cake mix

1 teaspoon espresso powder

2 pounds ricotta cheese

¾ cup sugar

1 teaspoon vanilla bean paste or vanilla extract

Frosting

1 cup milk

1 (3.4-ounce) box chocolate instant pudding mix

1 (8-ounce) tub mascarpone cheese, room temperature

1 (8-ounce) container frozen whipped topping, thawed

Shaved bittersweet dark chocolate curls for decorating

DIRECTIONS

1. Preheat the oven to 350°F. Grease a 9 × 13-inch baking dish.

2. *For the cake:* Prepare the cake batter according to the package directions, adding the espresso powder with the other ingredients. Pour into the baking dish.

3. In a large bowl, whisk the ricotta cheese, sugar, vanilla, and 4 eggs until smooth. Carefully pour the ricotta cheese mixture over the top of the cake batter. Spread to cover the cake.

4. Bake for 55 minutes to 1 hour or until a toothpick inserted in the center comes out clean. (The ricotta layer will sink while baking.) Transfer the pan to a wire rack and let the cake cool completely.

5. *For the frosting:* In a large bowl, whisk the milk and pudding mix until smooth. Carefully fold in the mascarpone cheese and whipped topping. Spread the frosting evenly over the cake and then sprinkle the chocolate curls on top. Refrigerate for at least 6 hours. Slice and serve.

Mint Patty Cake

Yield: Serves 12 | Prep Time: 25 minutes | Cook Time: 15 to 20 minutes

Maybe I've eaten one too many after-dinner mints when I've gone out to eat, but mint chocolate desserts just always seem to fit as a late-night dessert. This cake hits the spot when paired with a steaming mug of hot cocoa.

INGREDIENTS

Cake

2 cups all-purpose flour, plus extra for the pans

16 table-spoons (2 sticks) unsalted butter, softened

¼ cup cocoa powder

1 cup boiling water

10 whole miniature peppermint patties

½ cup buttermilk

2 large eggs

1 teaspoon baking soda

½ teaspoon vanilla bean paste or vanilla extract

¼ teaspoon mint extract

2 cups granulated sugar

¼ teaspoon kosher salt

Frosting

1 pound (4 sticks) unsalted butter, softened

2 tablespoons vanilla bean paste or vanilla extract

6 cups con-fectioners' sugar

⅛ teaspoon kosher salt

¼ cup heavy cream

¼ teaspoon mint extract

Mini pep-permint patties for decorating

DIRECTIONS

1. Preheat the oven to 350°F. Line two 9-inch round cake pans with parchment paper. Then grease and flour the pans.

2. *For the cake:* In a medium saucepan, melt the butter and mix in the cocoa powder. Pour in the boiling water, then set over low heat. Add the peppermint patties and stir until melted. Remove the pan from the heat and set aside for a few minutes to cool.

3. In a small bowl, whisk together the buttermilk, eggs, baking soda, vanilla, and mint extract. In a large bowl, whisk together the flour, sugar, and salt. Stir the butter-cocoa mixture into the flour mixture. Add the buttermilk mixture and stir to combine.

4. Divide the batter between the cake pans. Bake for 15 to 20 minutes or until the cake is set. Let the cakes cool in the pans for 10 minutes, then turn out onto a wire rack, remove the parchment, and let cool completely.

5. *For the frosting:* Using a hand mixer or a stand mixer fitted with the paddle attachment, beat the butter on medium speed until fluffy. Add the vanilla bean paste. Slowly add the confectioners' sugar and salt and beat until incorporated. Add the cream and mint extract and beat until fluffy.

6. Place one cake layer on a serving plate. Spread a generous amount of the frosting on top. Place the second layer on top of the first layer. Spread the frosting on the top and sides of the cake and smooth. Place the mini peppermint patties in a decorative pattern on top of the cake. Slice and serve.

Cinnamon Cream Cheese Apple Cake

Yield: Serves 12 to 15 | Prep Time: 15 minutes | Cook Time: 50 minutes to 1 hour

I like to think of this as the ultimate fall experience, with its combination of cinnamon and apples and the comforting density the cream cheese brings. In fact, it reminds me of a creamier version of coffee cake, so you can bet I've snuck in a piece or two before heading off to work.

INGREDIENTS

3 large apples, peeled, cored, and chopped

1 tablespoon lemon juice plus 1 teaspoon grated lemon zest

8 ounces cream cheese, room temperature

8 tablespoons (1 stick) unsalted butter, softened

1¾ cups granulated sugar

2 large eggs

1 tablespoon vanilla bean paste or vanilla extract

1½ cups all-purpose flour

2 teaspoons baking powder

¼ teaspoon kosher salt

½ cup chopped walnuts

⅓ cup packed light brown sugar

2 teaspoons ground cinnamon

1 teaspoon ground cardamom

DIRECTIONS

1. Preheat the oven to 350°F. Grease a 9 × 13-inch baking dish.

2. In a medium bowl, toss the chopped apples with the lemon juice.

3. Using a hand mixer or a stand mixer fitted with the paddle attachment, beat the cream cheese and butter on medium speed for 1 minute, then beat in the granulated sugar until fluffy. Add the eggs, one at a time, and beat until creamy. Beat in the vanilla and lemon zest.

4. In a small bowl, whisk together the flour, baking powder, and salt. On low speed, add the flour mixture to the cream cheese mixture and mix until incorporated. Fold the apples into the batter. Pour the batter into the baking dish.

5. In a small bowl, combine the walnuts, brown sugar, cinnamon, and cardamom. Sprinkle the mixture over the top of the cake batter.

6. Bake for 50 minutes to 1 hour or until the cake is golden and a toothpick inserted in the center comes out clean. Let cool in the pan, slice, and serve.

Glazed Rum Cake

Yield: Serves 8 to 10 | Prep Time: 20 minutes | Cook Time: 55 minutes to 1 hour 5 minutes

Rum cake is most commonly found in tropical locations in the Caribbean. My husband and I ordered some once when we were on vacation, and every time I've had it since, it's brought me right back to the palm trees and soft ocean breeze.

INGREDIENTS

Cake

1 cup chopped pecans

3 cups all-purpose flour

1 (3.4-ounce) box vanilla instant pudding mix

2 teaspoons baking powder

½ teaspoon baking soda

½ teaspoon kosher salt

16 tablespoons (2 sticks) unsalted butter, softened

1½ cups sugar

½ cup canola or vegetable oil

4 large eggs

½ cup light rum

2 teaspoons vanilla bean paste or vanilla extract

Butter Rum Glaze

8 tablespoons (1 stick) unsalted butter

1 cup sugar

¼ cup light rum

DIRECTIONS

1. Preheat the oven to 350°F. Grease a 12-cup Bundt pan.

2. *For the cake:* Sprinkle the pecans evenly in the bottom of the Bundt pan.

3. In a medium bowl, whisk together the flour, pudding mix, baking powder, baking soda, and salt. Using a hand mixer or a stand mixer fitted with the paddle attachment, beat the butter on medium speed until creamy. Beat in the sugar until light and fluffy. Reduce the speed to low and add the oil, eggs, rum, and vanilla. Slowly add the flour mixture and beat until well incorporated. Pour the batter into the Bundt pan over the nuts.

4. Bake for 55 minutes to 1 hour 5 minutes or until the cake is golden and a toothpick inserted in the center comes out clean. Set aside while you make the glaze.

5. *For the butter rum glaze:* In a small saucepan, combine the butter, sugar, rum, and ¼ cup water. Bring the mixture to a boil over medium heat and cook for 4 to 5 minutes, stirring and being careful not to burn the mixture. Remove from heat and let sit for 5 minutes.

6. Poke holes in the still-hot cake with a wooden skewer or fork.

7. Pour ¼ of the rum glaze over the cake and let seep in for 5 to 10 minutes. Invert the cake onto a serving plate. Poke holes over the top of the cake and pour another ¼ of the rum glaze over the cake. After some glaze has seeped in, drizzle another ¼ over the cake. Let the cake cool.

8. Slice the cake and serve with the remaining rum glaze for guests to drizzle over their slices.

Classic Chocolate Cake

Yield: Serves 8 to 10 | Prep Time: 30 minutes | Cook Time: 30 to 35 minutes

Whenever I'm in doubt about what kind of cake to make for guests, I know I can fall back on this classic chocolate cake recipe. The rich coffee taste in the cake makes this more sophisticated than the average box mix, but the soft, delicate texture makes it a reliable hit.

INGREDIENTS

Cake

2 cups granulated sugar

1¾ cups all-purpose flour

¾ cup plus 1 tablespoon cocoa powder

2 teaspoons baking soda

1 teaspoon baking powder

1 teaspoon kosher salt

1 cup buttermilk

1 cup strong black coffee

2 large eggs

½ cup vegetable oil

2 teaspoons vanilla bean paste or vanilla extract

Chocolate Frosting

16 tablespoons (2 sticks) unsalted butter, softened

3½ cups confectioners' sugar, plus extra if needed

½ cup cocoa powder

1 teaspoon espresso powder

¼ cup heavy cream, plus extra if needed

2 teaspoons vanilla bean paste or vanilla extract

½ teaspoon kosher salt

Malted milk balls and chocolate sprinkles for decorating

DIRECTIONS

1. Preheat the oven to 350°F. Line two 9-inch round cake pans with parchment paper and lightly grease the parchment paper and sides of the pans.

2. *For the cake:* Using a hand mixer or a stand mixer fitted with the whisk attachment, combine the sugar, flour, cocoa powder, baking soda, baking powder, and salt on low speed. Add the buttermilk, coffee, eggs, oil, and vanilla. Increase the speed to medium and beat for 2 to 3 minutes until well incorporated.

3. Divide the batter between the cake pans. Bake for 30 to 35 minutes or until a toothpick inserted in the center comes out clean.

4. Let the cakes cool in the pans for 10 minutes, then turn out onto a wire rack, remove the parchment, and let cool completely.

5. *For the frosting:* Using a hand mixer or a stand mixer fitted with the paddle attachment, beat the butter on medium speed for 1 to 2 minutes, until light and fluffy. Reduce the speed to low and gradually add the confectioners' sugar, cocoa powder, and espresso powder; beat until incorporated. Add the cream, vanilla, and salt, then increase the speed to medium and beat for 3 to 4 minutes until the frosting has a spreadable consistency. Add more sugar if the frosting needs to be a bit firmer or add additional cream to thin it out.

6. Place a cake layer on a serving plate. Spread the top with some of the frosting. Place the second cake layer on top. Frost the top and sides of the cake. Arrange the malted milk balls in a pretty pattern on top and add the chocolate sprinkles all over. Slice and serve.

No-Bake Chocolate Éclair Cake

Yield: Serves 12 | Prep Time: 15 minutes | Chill Time: 2 hours for ganache plus 8 hours for cake

I live in the Chicago suburbs, where there's an incredible restaurant chain called Portillo's. While they're best known for their Italian beef sandwiches, I've always been fond of their slices of chocolate éclair cake. This copycat version captures the rich but not-too-heavy texture of the dessert I've come to love.

INGREDIENTS

1½ cups heavy cream

12 ounces bittersweet dark chocolate, chopped

1 (14.4-ounce) box honey graham crackers

3 cups milk

2 (3.4-ounce) boxes French vanilla instant pudding mix

1 (12-ounce) container frozen whipped topping, thawed

DIRECTIONS

1. Heat the cream in the microwave or on the stovetop just until simmering. Place the chocolate in a heatproof bowl, pour the hot cream over the chocolate, and let stand for 2 to 3 minutes, then stir until smooth. Cover and let stand at room temperature for 2 hours, then whisk again.

2. Line the bottom of a 9 × 13-inch baking dish with one sleeve of the graham crackers.

3. In a large bowl, whisk the milk and pudding mix until thickened and smooth. Fold in the whipped topping.

4. Spread half of the pudding mixture over the graham crackers. Repeat the layers with another sleeve of graham crackers and the remaining pudding mixture. Top with the last sleeve of graham crackers, then spread with the chocolate ganache.

5. Refrigerate for 8 hours. Slice and serve.

NOTES

You can use a 16-ounce container of chocolate frosting instead of the chocolate ganache.

5

Dump Cakes, Poke Cakes, and Mug Cakes

Dump cakes are a last-minute lifesaver because you just need to throw all the ingredients into one dish, and you're good to go. I love serving the Apple Pie Dump Cake with Pecan Topping (page 124) in the fall just as the temperature starts to get a bit crisp and the Piña Colada Dump Cake (page 131) in the summer, alongside my favorite fruity drink. These recipes generally take fewer than 10 minutes to prepare, so you have no excuse to skip making dessert.

Poke cakes are a brilliant invention because they ignore the conventions of layered desserts and give you all of your favorite flavors mixed together in one bite. To make a poke cake, you usually use the handle of a wooden spoon to poke holes in the baked cake and pour in your favorite filling, like caramel (as in the Chocolate Turtle Poke Cake on page 140) or pudding (as in the Banana Pudding Poke Cake on page 147). Feel free to play around with the cake and filling combinations in this chapter to come up with something brand new!

And while my husband and I both adore cakes, even we can't always handle the prospect of eating an entire cake all by ourselves. When we're looking for something more manageable, I turn to mug cakes, single-serving cakes you can microwave (or put in the oven!) in your favorite coffee mug, so we can get our cake fix without wasting ingredients.

Apple Pie Dump Cake
with Pecan Topping

Yield: Serves 16 | Prep Time: 10 minutes | Cook Time: 40 to 45 minutes

Combining shortcut ingredients like cake mix and pie filling is one of my favorite behind-the-scenes party tricks. It's so much easier to use a prepared filling than to peel, core, and chop up a bunch of apples (and you won't even be able to tell the difference).

INGREDIENTS

1 (21-ounce) can apple pie filling

1 (16.5-ounce) box white cake mix

3 large eggs

½ cup vegetable oil

⅓ cup chopped pecans

¼ cup packed dark brown sugar

¼ teaspoon ground cinnamon

¼ teaspoon ground cardamom

½ teaspoon minced crystallized ginger

Caramel sauce for serving

DIRECTIONS

1. Preheat the oven to 350°F. Grease a 9 × 13-inch baking dish.

2. Place the apple filling in a large bowl. Break up the apple pieces with a spoon or fork.

3. Add the cake mix, eggs, and oil. Using a hand mixer or stand mixer fitted with the whisk attachment, beat for 2 minutes on medium speed until combined. Pour the batter into the baking dish.

4. In a small bowl, mix the pecans, brown sugar, cinnamon, cardamom, and ginger. Sprinkle the mixture over the cake.

5. Bake the cake for 40 to 45 minutes or until the cake is golden and a toothpick inserted in the center comes out clean. Let cool in the pan for 5 minutes. Slice and serve with caramel sauce.

Hubby's Favorite Dump Cake

Yield: Serves 8 | Prep Time: 5 minutes | Cook Time: 25 to 30 minutes

I can make my husband the fanciest cake around, with ganache and fondant and painstaking attention to detail, but I think he'll still love this one the best. I think it's the combination of textures that he loves—the smooth, juicy fruit paired with the nutty crunch of the almonds.

INGREDIENTS

1 (20-ounce) can crushed pineapple with juice

1 (21-ounce) can cherry pie filling

1 teaspoon rum extract

¾ cup chopped almonds

1 (15.25-ounce) box yellow cake mix

8 tablespoons (1 stick) unsalted butter, cut into cubes

Vanilla ice cream or whipped cream for serving

DIRECTIONS

1. Preheat the oven to 350°F. Lightly grease a 9 × 13-inch baking dish.

2. Spread the crushed pineapple in the baking dish, then spread the cherry filling over the pineapple. Sprinkle the rum extract over the cherry filling. Sprinkle ½ cup of the almonds over the filling. Sprinkle the cake mix evenly over the nuts and then arrange the butter cubes on top. Sprinkle with the remaining ¼ cup almonds.

3. Bake for 25 to 30 minutes or until the cake is golden brown.

4. Serve warm with vanilla ice cream or whipped cream.

Funfetti Dump Cake

Yield: Serves 8 | Prep Time: 5 minutes | Cook Time: 20 minutes

The more colorful the dish, the more I love it. When I can entertain my friends and family with something that not only tastes good but looks beautiful on the table, then my job is done. This multicolored Funfetti cake achieves just that.

INGREDIENTS

1 cup milk

1 (3.4-ounce) box vanilla instant pudding mix

20 golden Oreos, broken in half

½ cup white chocolate chips

1 (15.25-ounce) box Funfetti cake mix

8 tablespoons (1 stick) unsalted butter, thinly sliced

½ cup rainbow sprinkles, plus more for decorating

DIRECTIONS

1. Preheat the oven to 350°F.

2. In a medium bowl, whisk the milk and pudding mix until thickened and smooth. Spread the pudding on the bottom of a 9-inch pie dish.

3. Top with the Oreos and chocolate chips. Add the cake mix and spread evenly. Arrange the butter slices evenly over the cake mix, then top with the sprinkles.

4. Bake for 20 minutes or until firm and completely baked through. Top with additional sprinkles. Let cool completely in the pan, then serve.

Piña Colada Dump Cake

Yield: Serves 10 | Prep Time: 10 minutes | Cook Time: 45 to 55 minutes

The smooth taste of coconut milk and coconut flakes makes this cake like a vacation in a baking dish. The spiced rum adds a bit of extra excitement.

INGREDIENTS

16 tablespoons (2 sticks) unsalted butter

2 (20-ounce) cans pineapple chunks, drained

¾ cup coconut milk

⅓ cup spiced rum

1 (15.25-ounce) box yellow cake mix

2 cups sweetened shredded coconut, plus toasted coconut for serving

Whipped cream for serving

Maraschino cherries for serving

DIRECTIONS

1. Preheat the oven to 350°F.

2. Melt 8 tablespoons of the butter and pour into a 9 × 13-inch baking dish. Stir in the pineapple, coconut milk, and rum. Sprinkle the cake mix evenly over the pineapple. Sprinkle the coconut on top of the cake mix. Cut the remaining 8 tablespoons butter into small cubes and scatter evenly over the coconut.

3. Bake the cake for 45 to 55 minutes or until the coconut is golden. Check the cake halfway through to make sure the coconut does not burn. If needed, cover with a piece of aluminum foil.

4. Serve warm or at room temperature with whipped cream, cherries, and toasted coconut.

NOTES

You can use fresh pineapple instead of canned, if you wish.

To toast the coconut, spread on a baking sheet and bake at 350°F for 5 to 10 minutes or until light golden brown.

Snickers Poke Cake

Yield: Serves 16 | Prep Time: 20 minutes plus 3 hours chill time | Cook Time: 25 to 45 minutes

While candy bars are enjoyable all on their own, they're twice as yummy when baked into a decadent treat. If you'd prefer to substitute your favorite candy bar, feel free to do so!

INGREDIENTS

1 (15.25-ounce) box devil's food cake mix

Vegetable oil as needed for the cake mix

Eggs as needed for the cake mix

1 (14-ounce) can sweetened condensed milk

1 (12.2-ounce) jar caramel sauce, plus extra for drizzling

½ cup bittersweet chocolate chips

2 cups heavy cream

½ cup confectioners' sugar

1 teaspoon vanilla bean paste or vanilla extract

3 (1.86-ounce) Snickers candy bars, chopped

1 cup chopped roasted peanuts

Chocolate sauce for drizzling

DIRECTIONS

1. Preheat the oven and make the devil's food according to the package directions, using a 9 × 13-inch baking dish.

2. While the cake is baking, in a medium bowl, stir the condensed milk and caramel topping until combined.

3. Poke holes all over the hot cake using the handle of a wooden spoon or a thick wooden skewer. Pour the condensed milk mixture evenly over the cake. Let the cake cool completely in the pan, then sprinkle the chocolate chips over the cake.

4. Using a hand mixer or a stand mixer fitted with the whisk attachment, whip the cream, confectioners' sugar, and vanilla on medium speed until medium peaks form. Fold in the chopped Snickers. Spread over the cake. Sprinkle the top with the chopped peanuts. Drizzle caramel sauce and chocolate sauce over the cake. Refrigerate for 3 hours. Slice and serve.

Fall Pumpkin Dump Cake

Yield: Serves 15 | Prep Time: 10 minutes | Cook Time: 50 to 55 minutes

The combination of pumpkins and pecans make for an ideal quick treat when you're bringing out your favorite fall sweater and devouring your pumpkin spice treats.

INGREDIENTS

1 (15-ounce) can pumpkin puree

1 (5-ounce) can evaporated milk

3 large eggs

1 cup packed light brown sugar

2 teaspoons pumpkin-pie spice

1 teaspoon chopped crystallized ginger

½ teaspoon kosher salt

1 (15.25-ounce) box yellow cake mix

8 tablespoons (1 stick) unsalted butter, cut into thin slices

1 cup chopped pecans

1 teaspoon ground cinnamon

Bourbon Whipped Cream (optional; see Notes)

DIRECTIONS

1. Preheat the oven to 350°F. Grease a 9 × 13-inch baking dish.

2. In a medium bowl, mix together the pumpkin, evaporated milk, eggs, brown sugar, pumpkin-pie spice, ginger, and salt. Pour into the baking dish. Sprinkle the cake mix over the top. Top the cake with the butter slices. In a small bowl, combine the pecans and cinnamon. Sprinkle over the cake.

3. Bake for 50 to 55 minutes or until the cake is golden and a toothpick inserted in the center comes out clean.

4. Let the cake cool, then slice and serve with Bourbon Whipped Cream, if desired.

NOTES

To make Bourbon Whipped Cream, whisk 1 tablespoon bourbon into 1 cup whipped cream or whipped topping.

Slow Cooker Chocolate Lava Cake

Yield: Serves 12 | Prep Time: 15 minutes | Cook Time: 2 to 2½ hours on High

The gooier a dessert is, the yummier it tends to be. And believe me, this dessert is plenty gooey and yummy, thanks to the melted chocolate both on top and on the inside.

INGREDIENTS

1 (15.25-ounce) box chocolate cake mix

3 large eggs

3¼ cups milk

½ cup vegetable oil

½ teaspoon espresso powder

1 (3.4-ounce) box chocolate instant pudding mix

1 cup semisweet chocolate chips

1 cup bittersweet chocolate chips

Whipped cream for serving

Fresh raspberries for serving

DIRECTIONS

1. Lightly coat a 6-quart slow cooker with cooking spray.

2. In a large bowl, whisk together the cake mix, eggs, 1¼ cups of the milk, the oil, and espresso powder until smooth. Pour the mixture into the slow cooker. Beat the pudding mix with the remaining 2 cups milk until combined, then pour over the cake batter. Sprinkle the chocolate chips over the pudding layer. Do not stir.

3. Cover and cook for 2 to 2½ hours on High or until the sides of the cake are set and the middle is gooey.

4. Serve with whipped cream and raspberries.

Slow Cooker
Vanilla-Caramel Poke Cake

Yield: Serves 8 to 10 | Prep Time: 15 minutes, plus 1 to 2 hours chill time | Cook Time: 2 to 3 hours on High

My cooking friends all make fun of me because they think it's absurd that my favorite flavor in the entire world is vanilla. When you have a vanilla dessert as sweet and velvety-rich as this, with pudding oozing from the middle, it's hard to make an argument against it. And the dulce de leche complements the vanilla to perfection with its smooth, caramel flavor.

INGREDIENTS

1 (15.25-ounce) box white cake mix

Vegetable oil as needed for the cake mix

Eggs or egg whites as needed for the cake mix

1 (5.1-ounce) box instant vanilla pudding mix

2 cups milk, cold

1 (14-ounce) can dulce de leche, plus extra for drizzling

DIRECTIONS

1. Coat a 6-quart slow cooker with cooking spray. Prepare the vanilla cake batter according to the package directions and pour into the slow cooker.

2. Cover and cook on High for 2 to 3 hours or until the cake is golden and a toothpick inserted in the center comes out clean.

3. Remove the insert from the slow cooker and place on a wire rack. Use the handle of a wooden spoon to poke holes all over the cake, about an inch apart.

4. Whisk together the pudding mix and milk until combined. Pour the pudding immediately over the cake (while it's still thin and hasn't had a chance to set), getting the pudding into each of the holes. Use the back of the spoon to help push the pudding into the holes as needed. Spread half of the can of dulce de leche over the pudding. (You can warm it in the microwave to make it easier to spread.) Let the insert cool to room temperature. Place the insert in the refrigerator for 1 to 2 hours.

5. Drizzle with the remaining dulce de leche. Slice and serve.

Chocolate Turtle Poke Cake

Yield: Serves 12 | Prep Time: 15 minutes, plus 1 hour chill time | Cook Time: 30 to 35 minutes

The caramel filling adds a deliciously moist texture to the already-soft cake. The sweetened condensed milk thins out the caramel, so it's better able to squeeze into every nook and cranny.

INGREDIENTS

1 (15.25-ounce) box chocolate cake mix

Vegetable oil as needed for the cake mix

Eggs as needed for the cake mix

1 (14-ounce) can sweetened condensed milk

½ cup caramel sauce, plus extra for drizzling

1 (8-ounce) container frozen whipped topping, thawed

1 cup chopped pecans

½ cup mini chocolate chips

DIRECTIONS

1. Preheat the oven and make the chocolate cake according to the package directions, using a 9 × 13-inch baking dish. Let the cake cool for 10 minutes. Using the handle of a wooden spoon, poke several holes all over the cake.

2. In a liquid measuring cup, combine the sweetened condensed milk and caramel sauce. Pour evenly over the top of the cake, using the back of the spoon to help push it into the holes. Refrigerate the cake for 1 hour.

3. Frost the top of the cake with the whipped topping. Sprinkle with the pecans and chocolate chips. Drizzle the top with caramel sauce. Slice and serve.

Oreo Pudding Poke Cake

Yield: Serves 12 | Prep Time: 20 minutes, plus 3 hours chill time | Cook Time: 30 to 35 minutes

The gooey cookies and cream center tastes so much like the center of an Oreo cookie, it's almost unbelievable. If I'm feeling especially indulgent, I'll even have a scoop of cookies 'n' cream ice cream on the side!

INGREDIENTS

1 (15.25-ounce) box devil's food cake mix

Vegetable oil as needed for the cake mix

Eggs as needed for the cake mix

2 cups milk

2 (4.2-ounce) boxes cookies 'n' cream instant pudding mix (see Notes)

1 (8-ounce) container frozen whipped topping, thawed

8 Oreos, crushed

DIRECTIONS

1. Preheat the oven and make the devil's food cake according to the package directions, using a 9 × 13-inch baking dish.

2. When the cake is done baking, use the handle of a wooden spoon to poke several holes all over the cake, making sure the holes go all the way to the bottom. Whisk the milk and pudding mix until thickened and smooth. Let sit for 2 minutes. Pour the pudding over the cake, spreading with the back of the wooden spoon to help push the pudding into the holes. Refrigerate for 3 hours.

3. Spread the whipped topping evenly over the cake and sprinkle with the crushed Oreos. Scoop and serve.

NOTES

A combination of 1 (4.2-ounce) box of cookies 'n' cream instant pudding and 1 (3.4-ounce) box of chocolate instant pudding can be used instead.

Strawberry Jell-O Poke Cake

Yield: Serves 12 | Prep Time: 20 minutes, plus 3 hours chill time | Cook Time: 20 to 45 minutes

The power of box mixes really comes into play when you make this triple mix dessert. The trifecta of cake mix, gelatin mix, and pudding mix all come together to create a super-simple dish that is worthy of a bakery.

INGREDIENTS

Cake

1 (15.25-ounce) box white cake mix

Vegetable oil as needed for the cake mix

Egg whites as needed for the cake mix

1 (3-ounce) box strawberry gelatin mix

1 cup boiling water

Topping

1 (3.3-ounce) box white chocolate instant pudding mix

⅓ cup milk

¼ teaspoon rum extract

1 (8-ounce) container frozen whipped topping, thawed

Fresh strawberries, hulled and sliced, for serving

DIRECTIONS

1. *For the cake:* Preheat the oven and make the white cake according to the package directions, using a 9 × 13-inch baking dish. Let it cool in the pan for about 30 minutes. Using the handle of a wooden spoon, poke holes all over the cake, making sure the holes go all the way to the bottom.

2. Whisk the gelatin mix with the boiling water until the powder is totally dissolved, about 2 minutes. Pour the mixture over the top of the cake. Refrigerate for 3 hours.

3. *For the topping:* When the cake is cold, whisk the pudding mix, milk, and rum extract until thickened and smooth. Fold in the whipped topping. Spread the mixture over the cake and top with half of the strawberries. Slice the cake and serve with the remaining strawberries.

Banana Pudding Poke Cake

Yield: Serves 9 to 12 | Prep Time: 30 minutes, plus 2 hours chill time | Cook Time: 30 to 35 minutes

Banana desserts remind me of old-fashioned soda shops where you could get an elaborate ice cream confection for only a quarter. That vintage vibe is brought to life with this recipe in a trendy poke-cake form.

INGREDIENTS

Cake

1 (15.25-ounce) box yellow cake mix

Vegetable oil as needed for the cake mix

Eggs as needed for the cake mix

4 cups milk

2 (3.4-ounce) boxes banana cream instant pudding mix

Topping

1½ cups heavy cream

2 tablespoons confectioners' sugar

1 teaspoon rum extract

20 vanilla wafers, crushed

1 banana, peeled and sliced

DIRECTIONS

1. *For the cake:* Preheat the oven and make the yellow cake according to the package directions, using a 9 × 13-inch baking dish. Let it cool in the baking dish for about 30 minutes. Using the handle of a wooden spoon, poke holes all over the cake, making sure the holes go to the bottom.

2. In a large bowl, whisk the milk and pudding mix until smooth. Pour the pudding over the cake, spreading with the back of the wooden spoon to help push the pudding into the holes. Refrigerate for about 2 hours, until the cake has absorbed the pudding and is set.

3. *For the topping:* Using a hand mixer or a stand mixer fitted with the whisk attachment, whip the cream and confectioners' sugar until medium-stiff peaks form. Fold in the rum extract. Spread the top of the cake evenly with the whipped cream. Sprinkle the crushed vanilla wafers over the whipped cream. Top with the banana slices. Slice the cake and serve.

Cannoli Poke Cake

Yield: Serves 12 | Prep Time: 20 minutes, plus 3 to 4 hours chill time | Cook Time: 30 to 35 minutes

I used to love going into bakeries and picking up pastries when I visited Italy, so anytime I can incorporate a cannoli-like dessert into my everyday cooking is a welcome treat.

INGREDIENTS

1 (15.25-ounce) box white cake mix

Vegetable oil as needed for the cake mix

Egg whites as needed for the cake mix

1 (14-ounce) can sweetened condensed milk

1½ cups ricotta cheese

1½ cups mascarpone cheese, room temperature

1 teaspoon orange extract

1 cup confectioners' sugar

½ teaspoon ground cinnamon

½ cup mini chocolate chips

½ cup finely chopped pistachios

Confectioners' sugar for dusting

DIRECTIONS

1. *For the cake:* Preheat the oven and make the white cake according to the package directions, using a 9 × 13-inch baking dish. Let it cool in the baking dish for about 30 minutes. Using the handle of a wooden spoon, poke holes all over the cake, making sure the holes go to the bottom. Reserve ½ cup of the sweetened condensed milk and pour the rest evenly over the cake. Refrigerate for 1 hour.

2. In a large bowl, stir the ricotta cheese, mascarpone cheese, and orange extract until smooth. Stir in the confectioners' sugar and cinnamon. Add the remaining sweetened condensed milk, and stir. Spread the frosting over the top of the cake. Sprinkle the chocolate chips and pistachios over the cake. Dust the top of the cake with confectioners' sugar. Refrigerate for 3 hours. Scoop and serve.

Carrot Cake Poke Cake

Yield: Serves 12 | Prep Time: 20 minutes, plus 8 hours chill time | Cook Time: 35 to 45 minutes

I'm generally in charge of bringing dessert to Easter dinner, and when I discovered this poke cake version of our spring favorite, my family was thrilled. The creamy pudding adds enough of an interesting twist to make it a talking point at the table but is familiar enough to avoid making waves.

INGREDIENTS

1 (15.25-ounce) box carrot cake mix

1 (3.4-ounce) box vanilla instant pudding mix

4 large eggs

1 cup sour cream

¾ cup vegetable oil

½ cup milk

1 (14-ounce) can sweetened condensed milk

2 cups heavy cream

5 tablespoons and 1 teaspoon cheesecake instant pudding mix

½ cup confectioners' sugar

Caramel sauce for drizzling

½ cup chopped pecans

DIRECTIONS

1. Preheat the oven to 350°F. Grease a 9 × 13-inch baking dish.

2. Using a hand mixer or a stand mixer fitted with the paddle attachment, beat the cake mix, vanilla pudding mix, eggs, sour cream, oil, and milk on medium speed until blended. Pour into the baking dish and bake for 35 to 45 minutes or until the cake is browned and a toothpick inserted in the center comes out clean.

3. Let the cake cool completely in the baking dish. Using the handle of a wooden spoon, poke holes over the entire cake. Pour the sweetened condensed milk over the cake and let it chill for 8 hours.

4. After the cake has set, using a hand mixer or a stand mixer with the whisk attachment, whip the heavy cream, cheesecake pudding mix, and confectioners' sugar until light and fluffy. Spread over the cake. Drizzle caramel sauce over the top and sprinkle with the chopped pecans. Slice and serve.

Snickerdoodle Mug Cake

Yield: Serves 1 | Prep Time: 5 minutes | Cook Time: 1 to 1½ minutes

Snickerdoodles are one of my favorite types of cookies—especially in the fall when cinnamon is at the peak of its popularity. I usually like to add a bit of whipped cream and extra cinnamon on top to really wrap up the flavor.

INGREDIENTS

6 tablespoons all-purpose flour

3 tablespoons sugar

½ teaspoon ground cinnamon

¼ teaspoon baking powder

¼ cup milk, room temperature

2 tablespoons salted butter, melted and cooled

½ teaspoon vanilla bean paste or vanilla extract

DIRECTIONS

1. In a small bowl, whisk together the flour, 2 tablespoons of the sugar, ¼ teaspoon of the cinnamon, and the baking powder until completely combined. Whisk in the milk, butter, and vanilla until the batter is smooth.

2. In a separate bowl, combine the remaining 1 tablespoon sugar and ¼ teaspoon cinnamon. Scoop a spoonful of batter into a 12-ounce microwave-safe mug, then sprinkle with a spoonful of cinnamon sugar. Alternate layers, ending with the cinnamon sugar.

3. Microwave on high for 1 to 1½ minutes or until the cake puffs up.

4. Let cool for a few minutes before serving.

Four-Ingredient Molten Nutella Lava Cake

Yield: Serves 1 | Prep Time: 5 minutes | Cook Time: 16 to 18 minutes

The first time I ever had a lava cake, I was astounded. I mean, why pour hot fudge on top when you can ensure that you get a forkful with each delectable bite of cake? This version is even better than most lava cakes because the soft center is the king of all dessert sauces: Nutella.

INGREDIENTS

¼ cup all-purpose flour

¼ cup Nutella

3 tablespoons milk

¼ teaspoon baking powder

DIRECTIONS

1. Preheat the oven to 350°F. In a 6-ounce oven-safe mug, combine the flour, Nutella, milk, and baking powder. Whisk vigorously with a fork until the batter is completely mixed and smooth.

2. Place the mug on a baking sheet. Bake for 16 to 18 minutes or until the cake is puffed up around the edges but the center looks dark and not completely set.

3. Let cool for a few minutes before eating.

Moist Vanilla Mug Cake

Yield: Serves 1 | Prep Time: 5 minutes | Cook Time: 2 minutes

Vanilla cakes provide the ideal palette to test out other flavors. I like to garnish this with whipped topping and berries, but you could add hot fudge sauce and candy bars, caramel sauce and nuts, or even Nutella and graham crackers. Make this treat your own!

INGREDIENTS

6 tablespoons all-purpose flour

2 tablespoons sugar

¼ teaspoon baking powder

⅛ teaspoon salt

6 tablespoons milk

½ tablespoon vanilla bean paste or vanilla extract

2 tablespoons unsalted butter, melted

Whipped topping

Fresh berries

DIRECTIONS

1. In a medium bowl, whisk together the flour, sugar, baking powder, and salt. In a small bowl, whisk together the milk and vanilla. Make a well in the center of the flour mixture, then pour the milk mixture into the center, followed by the melted butter. Whisk until no lumps remain and the batter is smooth and well combined.

2. Pour into a 12-ounce microwave-safe mug. Microwave on high for 2 minutes.

3. Let cool for a few minutes. Top with whipped topping and berries and eat.

Cookies 'n' Cream Mug Cake

Yield: Serves 1 | Prep Time: 5 minutes | Cook Time: 1 minute 40 seconds

Cookies and cream is one of those combinations that always reminds me of summer. I just picture a huge scoop of ice cream on top of a sugar cone under the blazing sunshine. This recipe satisfies my cravings when I don't have the tub of ice cream handy!

INGREDIENTS

¼ cup white chocolate chips

3 tablespoons milk

¼ cup all-purpose flour

¼ teaspoon baking powder

1½ teaspoons vegetable oil

2 chocolate sandwich cookies

DIRECTIONS

1. In a 12-ounce microwave-safe mug, combine the white chocolate chips and milk. Microwave on high for about 40 seconds or until the chocolate has melted. Whisk with a mini whisk until the chocolate is completely melted. Add the flour, baking powder, and oil and whisk until the batter is smooth.

2. Using a fork, smash the chocolate sandwich cookies into the batter until only small chunks of cookie remain.

3. Microwave on high for about 1 minute. Let the cake cool for a few minutes before eating.

Fudgy S'mores Mug Cake

Yield: Serves 1 | Prep Time: 5 minutes | Cook Time: 2 minutes

When it comes to s'mores, I say, the fudgier, the better! While some people double up on the marshmallows, I usually go for double the chocolate, and with the combination of a milk chocolate bar and cocoa powder, this mug cake achieves the same effect.

INGREDIENTS

3½ tablespoons unsalted butter

1½ ounces milk chocolate, chopped

2 tablespoons graham cracker crumbs

1 large egg

2 tablespoons sugar

½ teaspoon vanilla bean paste or vanilla extract

¼ cup all-purpose flour

2 tablespoons cocoa powder

⅛ teaspoon baking powder

Large marshmallows

DIRECTIONS

1. In a small microwave-safe bowl, combine 3 tablespoons of the butter and one-third of the chocolate. Microwave on high for 20 to 30 seconds or until melted. Set aside. In a 12-ounce microwave-safe mug, microwave the remaining ½ tablespoon butter with the graham cracker crumbs until melted and stir until moistened. Press the crumb mixture into the bottom of the mug.

2. In a small bowl, whisk the egg, sugar, and vanilla until smooth. Add the flour, cocoa, and baking powder and stir until a thick batter forms. Pour in the melted chocolate mixture, and stir to combine. Fold in the remaining chocolate. Pour the mixture on top of the graham cracker crust. Top with the marshmallows and microwave for 1 minute and 20 seconds or until puffy. Remove and top with additional marshmallows if desired. Let cool for a few minutes before eating.

The Best Pumpkin Mug Cake

Yield: Serves 1 | Prep Time: 5 minutes | Cook Time: 1½ minutes

When September and October roll around, I load up on every pumpkin and apple treat imaginable because they're on sale and so fitting for the season. When I have a craving for something pumpkin during the other ten months of the year, this is the recipe I turn to for a little fall-like pick-me-up.

INGREDIENTS

6 tablespoons vanilla cake mix

2 tablespoons canned pumpkin puree

1 tablespoon milk

1 tablespoon vegetable oil

1 teaspoon pumpkin-pie spice

Vanilla ice cream for serving

DIRECTIONS

1. In a standard mason jar or 12-ounce mug, use a fork to whisk the cake mix, pumpkin puree, milk, oil, and pumpkin-pie spice until smooth.

2. Microwave on high for 1 minute and 30 seconds. Let cool for a few minutes. Top with ice cream and eat.

6

Special Occasion Cakes

Holidays and formal celebrations are just another excuse for making
more cakes. Dessert becomes part of the décor, creating a richer
party atmosphere and bringing the whole event together.

Lemon Chiffon Layer Cake

Yield: Serves 8 to 10 | Prep Time: 20 minutes plus 30 minutes chill time | Cook Time: 30 to 35 minutes

This light, lemony cake is an elegant dish for sweet daytime affairs like baby showers or afternoon tea. The lemon curd filling is my favorite part because it's not too sweet and not too tart.

INGREDIENTS

Lemon Cream Frosting

1½ cups heavy cream

3 tablespoons sugar

3 tablespoons lemon curd

Cake

6 large eggs, separated

½ cup vegetable or canola oil

2 teaspoons grated lemon zest plus 2 teaspoons lemon juice

1¾ cups cake flour

1½ cups sugar

1 tablespoon baking powder

1 teaspoon kosher salt

½ teaspoon cream of tartar

1 cup jarred lemon curd

DIRECTIONS

1. Preheat the oven to 350°F. Line three 8-inch round cake pans with parchment paper and very lightly coat with cooking spray.

2. *For the lemon cream frosting:* Using a hand mixer or stand mixer with a chilled bowl and whisk attachment, whip the heavy cream with the sugar until stiff peaks form. Fold in the lemon curd. Refrigerate until ready to use.

3. *For the cake:* In a medium bowl, whisk together the egg yolks, oil, lemon zest and juice, and ¾ cup cold water. In a large bowl, whisk together the flour, 1 cup of the sugar, the baking powder, and salt. Make a well in the center of the flour mixture and add the egg yolk mixture; whisk until smooth.

4. Using a hand mixer or a stand mixer fitted with the whisk attachment, mix the egg whites and cream of tartar on low speed until light and foamy. Increase the speed to medium. Gradually add the remaining ½ cup sugar and whip until stiff peaks form. Stir in about ⅓ of the whipped egg whites into the cake batter. Fold in the remaining egg white mixture. Divide the batter into the cake pans.

5. Bake for 30 to 35 minutes or until the cake is golden and a toothpick inserted in the center comes out clean. Let the cakes cool in the pans for 10 minutes, then turn out onto a wire rack, remove the parchment, and let cool completely.

6. Place 1 cake layer on a serving plate. Spread ½ cup of the lemon curd evenly over the top of the cake. Set the second layer on top of the first, then spread the remaining ½ cup lemon curd on top. Place the last cake layer on top.

7. Spread the frosting on the top and sides of the cake.

8. Refrigerate the cake for 30 minutes before slicing and serving.

Dreamsicle Cake

Yield: Serves 10 to 12 | Prep Time: 25 minutes | Cook Time: 30 to 35 minutes

Anytime I hear "Dreamsicle," I'm immediately brought back to my childhood. I'd run down the street chasing the ice cream truck, hoping to collect something fruity and sticky to enjoy on a hot summer day. The combination of a bright citrus flavor and a smooth, creamy sweet is just as delightful today as it was all those years ago.

INGREDIENTS

1 (16.5-ounce) box orange cake mix

Vegetable oil as needed for the cake mix

Eggs as needed for the cake mix

¼ cup frozen orange juice concentrate, thawed

16 tablespoons (2 sticks) unsalted butter, thinly sliced, cold

1 pound cream cheese, cut into cubes, cold

1 teaspoon vanilla bean paste or vanilla extract

1 teaspoon orange extract

½ teaspoon kosher salt

6 cups confectioners' sugar

Orange gel food coloring (optional)

Sliced oranges and grated orange peel

DIRECTIONS

1. Preheat the oven according to the cake mix package directions. Make the orange cake, substituting the orange juice concentrate for ¼ cup of the water called for, and using two 8-inch round cake pans that have been greased and lined with parchment paper.

2. Let the cakes cool in the pans for 10 minutes, then turn out onto a wire rack, remove the parchment, and let cool completely.

3. Using a hand mixer or a stand mixer fitted with the paddle attachment, beat the butter on medium speed until smooth. Add the cream cheese and beat on medium speed until smooth and fluffy. Add the vanilla, orange extract, and salt. Reduce the speed to low and gradually beat in the confectioners' sugar until incorporated. Increase the speed to medium-high and beat until fluffy. Add a few drops of orange gel coloring, if desired.

4. Place 1 cake layer on a serving plate. Spread a generous amount of the frosting over the cake. Set the second cake layer in place and frost the top and sides of the cake. Decorate with grated orange peel and sliced oranges. Slice and serve.

Southern Caramel Cake

Yield: Serves 12 | Prep Time: 25 minutes | Cook Time: 25 to 30 minutes

I've been fortunate enough to attend the Kentucky Derby a few times with Rick Tramonto, cookbook author and co-founder of the famous Chicago restaurant Tru. One of my favorite parts is sampling all the Southern cuisine that's offered, especially the desserts! Anytime I can get my hands on a slice of caramel cake, I'm thrilled. This shortcut version brings me back to the Derby every time.

INGREDIENTS

Cake

1 (15.25-ounce) box yellow butter cake mix

Vegetable oil as needed for the cake mix

Eggs as needed for the cake mix

Icing

2¼ cups packed light brown sugar

8 tablespoons (1 stick) unsalted butter

7 tablespoons evaporated milk, plus extra as needed

1 teaspoon vanilla bean paste or vanilla extract

Pecan halves for decorating (optional)

DIRECTIONS

1. *For the cake:* Preheat the oven and make the yellow butter cake according to the package directions, using two 9-inch round cake pans that have been lined with parchment paper.

2. Let the cakes cool in the pans for 10 minutes, then turn out onto a wire rack, remove the parchment, and let cool completely.

3. *For the icing:* In a medium saucepan, combine the brown sugar, butter, evaporated milk, and vanilla. Bring to a boil over medium-high heat. Stir until smooth, reduce the heat to low, and let the mixture gently boil for 7 to 8 minutes. Remove from the heat and let it cool for 5 minutes. Transfer to a bowl and whip the icing for 2 to 3 minutes until it becomes thick.

4. Place 1 cake layer on a serving plate. Working quickly, spread an even layer of the icing over the cake. Set the second cake layer in place. Spread the icing on the top and the sides of the cake. If the icing starts to become too firm to spread, return it to low heat and add a tablespoon or two of evaporated milk and stir until smooth again. Whip until it becomes thick.

5. Top the cake with pecans, if desired. Slice and serve.

Strawberry–Chocolate Mousse Cake

Yield: Serves 8 to 10 | Prep Time: 15 minutes plus 6 hours chill time | Cook Time: 45 minutes

I wanted something sweet and romantic and this combination of juicy strawberries and rich chocolate fit the bill.

INGREDIENTS

Chocolate Cake

1 cup sugar

¾ cup plus 2 tablespoons all-purpose flour

6 tablespoons cocoa powder

¾ teaspoon baking powder

¾ teaspoon baking soda

½ teaspoon salt

½ cup milk

¼ cup vegetable oil

1 large egg

1 teaspoon vanilla bean paste or vanilla extract

½ cup boiling water

Chocolate Ganache

⅔ cup heavy cream

5½ ounces semisweet chocolate, chopped

Chocolate Mousse

3 cups milk

1 (5.9-ounce) box instant chocolate pudding mix

1 (8-ounce) container frozen whipped topping, thawed

1 pound fresh strawberries

DIRECTIONS

1. Preheat the oven to 350°F. Grease a 9-inch round cake pan and line with parchment paper.

2. *For the chocolate cake:* Combine the sugar, flour, cocoa, baking powder, baking soda, and salt on low speed. Add the milk, oil, egg, and vanilla and mix on medium speed for 2 minutes. Add the boiling water and mix until combined.

3. Pour the batter into the cake pan and bake for 25 to 35 minutes. Let cool in the pan for 10 minutes, then turn out onto a wire rack, and let cool completely. Place on a serving plate.

4. *For the chocolate ganache:* Heat the cream just until simmering. Place the chocolate in a heatproof bowl, pour in the hot cream, and let stand for 2 to 3 minutes, then stir until smooth. Let cool, then spread on top of the cake.

5. *For the chocolate mousse filling:* In a medium bowl, whisk the milk and pudding until thickened. Fold in the topping.

6. Set the ring from a 9-inch springform pan around the cake, then spread ½ cup of the chocolate mousse on the cake. Stand the strawberries around the edge. Transfer the remaining mousse to a pastry bag and fill in all the gaps, then pipe the rest in the center and smooth the top. Refrigerate for 6 hours to set. Run a thin knife around the cake and release the ring from the springform pan.

7. Scatter additional strawberries on top and garnish with extra chocolate. Slice and serve.

Black Forest Cake

Yield: Serves 8 to 10 | Prep Time: 15 minutes, plus 30 minutes chill time | Cook Time: 45 minutes

Black Forest cake is named for the area in southwest Germany where it originated. That particular area features cherries as one of its main crops, and cherries take center stage with this recipe.

INGREDIENTS

2 (15.2-ounce) boxes chocolate cake mix

Vegetable oil as needed for the cake mix

Eggs as needed for the cake mix

1 (8-ounce) container frozen whipped topping, thawed

1 (10-ounce) jar maraschino cherries, drained

2 (16-ounce) containers chocolate frosting

1 (21-ounce) can cherry pie filling

4 ounces bittersweet dark chocolate

DIRECTIONS

1. Preheat the oven and make the chocolate cake according to the package directions, using four 8-inch round cake pans (two for each cake mix). Let the cakes cool in the pans for 10 minutes, then turn out onto a wire rack to cool completely.

2. Place 1 cake layer on a serving plate and spread one-quarter of the whipped topping on top. Scatter one-third of the maraschino cherries over the topping. Repeat twice more and then set the fourth cake layer on top. Refrigerate the cake for 30 minutes.

3. Frost the top and sides of the cake with the chocolate frosting. Pipe the remaining whipped topping on the top of the cake around the edge. Spoon the cherry pie filling inside the ring of whipped topping. Using a vegetable peeler, shave chocolate from the chocolate bar and pat it onto the sides of the cake. Slice and serve.

Gooiest Butter Cake

Yield: Serves 15 | Prep Time: 15 minutes | Cook Time: 45 to 50 minutes

Butter cake is a Southern staple that I adore. It has a dense texture and rich flavor that make it one of my favorite treats. This particular recipe uses a shortcut by incorporating cake mix, so it's simpler than ever to enjoy anytime.

INGREDIENTS

1 (15.25-ounce) box yellow cake mix

12 tablespoons (1½ sticks) unsalted butter, melted

3 large eggs

8 ounces cream cheese, room temperature

1 teaspoon vanilla bean paste or vanilla extract

4 cups confectioners' sugar, plus extra for dusting

DIRECTIONS

1. Preheat the oven to 350°F. Grease a 9 × 13-inch baking dish.

2. Using a hand mixer or a stand mixer fitted with the paddle attachment, beat the cake mix with ½ cup of the melted butter and 1 egg. Press the mixture into the baking dish.

3. In a medium bowl, beat the cream cheese, the remaining 2 eggs, the remaining ¼ cup melted butter, and the vanilla until smooth.

4. Beat in the confectioners' sugar until mixed in. Spread the mixture over the batter.

5. Bake for 45 to 50 minutes or until the cake is golden brown. The center will be a bit gooey.

6. Let it cool in the pan and dust the top with confectioners' sugar. Slice and serve.

Chocolate Oreo Cake

Yield: Serves 8 to 10 | Prep Time: 20 minutes | Cook Time: 25 to 28 minutes

The Oreo-frosting combination is certainly the highlight of this cake. The crunch of the Oreo cookies against the creamy frosting and soft, fluffy cake is a heavenly combination.

INGREDIENTS

2 cups all-purpose flour

2 cups sugar

¾ cup cocoa powder

2 teaspoons baking soda

1 teaspoon salt

1 cup milk

1 cup vegetable oil

2 large eggs

1 teaspoon vanilla bean paste or vanilla extract

1 cup boiling water

2 cups crushed Oreos, plus chopped Oreos for decorating

2 (12-ounce) containers vanilla frosting

DIRECTIONS

1. Preheat the oven to 300°F. Line two 9-inch round cake pans with parchment paper and grease the sides.

2. In a large bowl, whisk together the flour, sugar, cocoa powder, baking soda, and salt. Add the milk, oil, eggs, and vanilla and whisk until smooth. Add the boiling water. Mix well to combine.

3. Divide the batter between the cake pans and bake for 25 to 28 minutes or until a toothpick comes out with a few crumbs. Let the cakes cool in the pans for 10 minutes, then turn out onto a wire rack, remove the parchment, and let cool completely.

4. In a medium bowl, combine the crushed Oreos with the frosting.

5. Once the cakes are cool, flatten the tops with a large serrated knife.

6. Place 1 cake layer on a serving plate. Spread half of the frosting on top in an even layer.

7. Set the second cake layer in place and spread the rest of the frosting on top and around the sides of the cake. Sprinkle chopped Oreos on the cake, slice, and serve.

Peanut Butter Cup Cake

Yield: Serves 8 to 10 | Prep Time: 30 minutes | Cook Time: 25 to 35 minutes

My husband loves sweets, so it was no surprise when we started dating to find a candy drawer in his kitchen. I would sneak mini peanut butter cups to munch on all the time, so I was thrilled when I got to try this recipe.

INGREDIENTS

Cake

1 (15.25-ounce) box white cake mix

Vegetable oil as needed for the cake mix

Egg whites as needed for the cake mix

¼ cup creamy peanut butter

Peanut Butter Buttercream

16 tablespoons (2 sticks) unsalted butter, softened

1 cup creamy peanut butter

3 cups confectioners' sugar

1 teaspoon vanilla bean paste or vanilla extract

¼ cup heavy cream, plus extra as needed

2 cups peanut butter cups, quartered

1 cup chocolate syrup

DIRECTIONS

1. *For the cake:* Preheat the oven to 350°F. Line two 9-inch round cake pans with parchment paper and grease the parchment.

2. Prepare the white cake according to the package directions. Add the peanut butter and stir to combine. Divide the batter between the cake pans and bake for 25 to 35 minutes or until the cake is golden and a toothpick inserted in the center comes out clean.

3. Let the cakes cool in the pans for 20 minutes, then turn out onto a wire rack, remove the parchment, and let cool completely.

4. *For the peanut butter buttercream:* Using a hand mixer or a stand mixer fitted with the paddle attachment, beat the butter and peanut butter on medium speed for 2 to 3 minutes until soft. Carefully add the confectioners' sugar in 3 to 4 batches. Beat in the vanilla, then add the heavy cream and beat until smooth. If the buttercream appears too stiff, add more cream.

5. Trim the tops of the cakes as necessary to level them. Remove excess crumbs.

6. Invert one cake layer onto a serving plate and spread a thin layer of frosting on top.

7. Set the second cake layer in place. Spread the remaining frosting on the top and sides of the cake. Top with peanut butter cups and drizzle with chocolate syrup. Slice and serve.

Pumpkin Angel Food Cake

Yield: Serves 12 | Prep Time: 15 minutes | Cook Time: 35 to 45 minutes

Pumpkin adds a bit more density than is usual with angel food cake, but it still maintains its signature softness. The cinnamon whipped cream topping is light as air and perfectly creamy.

INGREDIENTS

Angel Food Cake

1 cup canned pumpkin puree

1½ teaspoons pumpkin-pie spice

1 teaspoon vanilla bean paste or vanilla extract

¼ teaspoon crystallized ginger, chopped fine

1 (16-ounce) box angel food cake mix

Vegetable oil as needed for the cake mix

Egg whites as needed for the cake mix

Cinnamon Whipped Cream

1 cup heavy cream

2 tablespoons confectioners' sugar

1 teaspoon ground cinnamon

DIRECTIONS

1. Preheat the oven to 350°F.

2. *For the angel food cake:* In a small bowl, combine the pumpkin, pumpkin-pie spice, vanilla, and ginger. Set aside.

3. Prepare the angel food cake batter according to the package directions. Carefully fold the pumpkin mixture into the cake batter. Spoon the batter into an ungreased angel food cake pan.

4. Bake for 35 to 45 minutes or until the cake is golden and springs back when touched. Let the cake cool completely in the pan. Carefully remove the cake from the pan and set on a serving plate.

5. *For the cinnamon whipped cream:* Using a hand mixer or a stand mixer fitted with the whisk attachment, whip the cream with the confectioners' sugar and cinnamon until soft peaks form. Spread on top of the cake. Slice and serve.

Key Lime Angel Food Cake

Yield: Serves 8 | Prep Time: 20 minutes | Cook Time: 35 to 40 minutes

The key lime juice combined with the lightness of the angel food cake makes this a vacation-worthy dessert. The pistachio topping adds a delicate but distinct flavor for a particularly memorable dish.

INGREDIENTS

Cake

12 large egg whites (1½ cups), room temperature

2 tablespoons key lime juice

1½ teaspoons cream of tartar

½ teaspoon kosher salt

½ teaspoon grated lime zest

1½ cups granulated sugar

1 cup cake flour

Glaze

1 cup confectioners' sugar

3 tablespoons key lime juice

1 teaspoon grated lime zest

¼ cup finely chopped pistachios

DIRECTIONS

1. Preheat the oven to 350°F.

2. *For the cake:* Using a hand mixer or stand mixer fitted with the whisk attachment, beat the egg whites, key lime juice, cream of tartar, salt, and lime zest on high speed until stiff peaks form. Reduce the speed to low and slowly add the sugar until incorporated. Sprinkle a bit of the cake flour at a time over the egg white mixture and carefully fold in.

3. Spoon the batter into a 16-cup ungreased angel food cake pan and bake for 35 to 40 minutes or until the cake is golden and springs back when touched.

4. Invert the pan and let the cake cool completely in the pan. Carefully remove the cake from the pan and set on a serving plate.

5. *For the glaze:* In a small bowl, whisk together the confectioners' sugar, key lime juice, and lime zest. Drizzle the glaze over the cake and sprinkle the top with the pistachios. Slice and serve.

Hot Chocolate Cake

Yield: Serves 12 | Prep Time: 25 minutes | Cook Time: 28 to 32 minutes

Wintertime is filled with cozy movie nights with my husband and puppy, our mugs brimming with freshly made hot chocolate. I'm sure this cake is going to become part of our routine too!

INGREDIENTS

Cake

3 large eggs plus 1 large egg yolk

1⅓ cups dark hot chocolate (see Notes)

½ cup vegetable oil

1 (15.25-ounce) box chocolate cake mix

Ganache

½ cup heavy cream

¾ cup semisweet chocolate chips

Marshmallow Fluff

16 tablespoons (2 sticks) unsalted butter, softened

3 cups plus 3 tablespoons marshmallow crème

½ teaspoon vanilla bean paste or vanilla extract

2 cups confectioners' sugar

Mini marshmallows for decorating

DIRECTIONS

1. Preheat the oven to 350°F. Grease two 8-inch round cake pans. Line the pans with parchment paper.

2. *For the cake:* Using a hand mixer or a stand mixer fitted with the whisk attachment, whip the eggs and yolk, hot chocolate, and oil until blended. Gradually add the cake mix and whip until combined. Divide the batter between the cake pans. Bake for 28 to 32 minutes or until a toothpick inserted in the center comes out clean. Let the cakes cool in the pans for 10 minutes, then turn out onto a wire rack, remove the parchment, and let cool completely.

3. *For the ganache:* Heat the cream just until simmering. Place the chocolate chips in a heatproof bowl, pour the hot cream over them, and let stand for 2 to 3 minutes, then stir until smooth. Set aside to cool.

4. *For the marshmallow fluff:* Using a hand mixer or a stand mixer fitted with the paddle attachment, beat the butter on medium speed until light and fluffy. Add the marshmallow crème and vanilla and carefully mix into the butter. Gradually add in the confectioners' sugar and beat until combined.

5. Place 1 cake layer on a serving plate. Spread about half of the marshmallow fluff mixture over the top of the cake. Drizzle some of the chocolate ganache over the marshmallow fluff mixture, letting it drip over the side of the cake.

6. Place the second cake layer on top of the first. Spread the remaining marshmallow fluff mixture over the top until smooth. Drizzle the ganache over the top and sides of the cake.

7. Arrange a few handfuls of mini marshmallows on top of the cake. Using a kitchen torch, lightly brown the marshmallows. (If you do not have a torch, leave the marshmallows as is or dust with cocoa powder or graham cracker crumbs.) Slice and serve.

NOTES

Prepare this using dark hot chocolate powder, following the instructions on the container to get 1⅓ cups liquid.

Oreo Icebox Dessert

Yield: Serves 12　|　Prep Time: 15 minutes　|　Chill Time: 40 minutes plus 8 hours

This sticky, gooey mess of a dessert is guaranteed to be a favorite guilty pleasure. I've topped this dessert off with crushed Heath bars, but feel free to substitute your favorite candy bar.

INGREDIENTS

1 (15-ounce) package Oreos, crushed

6 tablespoons unsalted butter, melted

8 ounces cream cheese, room temperature

1 cup confectioners' sugar

1 (16-ounce) container frozen whipped topping, thawed

1 (5.1-ounce) box chocolate instant pudding mix

2 cups milk

1½ cups crushed Heath Toffee Bars

DIRECTIONS

1. Reserve ¼ cup crushed Oreos. In a medium bowl, mix the rest of the crushed Oreos with the melted butter. Press evenly into the bottom of a 9 × 13-inch baking dish.

2. In a medium bowl, mix together the cream cheese and confectioners' sugar until smooth. Fold in half of the whipped topping until blended. Spread evenly over the crushed Oreo layer. Refrigerate for 20 minutes.

3. In a large bowl, whisk together the pudding mix and milk until thickened and smooth. Spread over the cream cheese layer. Refrigerate for 20 minutes.

4. Spread the remaining whipped topping evenly over the pudding layer. Sprinkle with the reserved crushed Oreos and top with the crushed Heath bars.

5. Refrigerate for 8 hours. Slice and serve.

NOTES

We used a food processor to crush the Oreos, but you could also put them in a bag and crush them with a rolling pin.

Peanut Butter Lover's Icebox Cake

Yield: Serves 9 | Prep Time: 20 minutes | Chill Time: 8 hours

Peanut butter fanatics are going to go wild for this one. It has a triple helping of peanut butter provided by the sandwich cookies, peanut butter cups, and creamy peanut butter itself. I drizzle chocolate and caramel sauces on top, but if you want to amp up the peanut butter flavor even more, feel free to add peanut butter chips!

INGREDIENTS

½ cup creamy peanut butter

2 cups milk

1 (3.4-ounce) box cheesecake or vanilla instant pudding mix

26 peanut butter sandwich cookies, plus extra for decorating

1 (8-ounce) container frozen whipped topping, thawed

24 mini peanut butter cups, chopped, plus extra for decorating

Hot fudge sauce for drizzling

Caramel sauce for drizzling

DIRECTIONS

1. Line an 8-inch square baking dish with parchment paper. Put the peanut butter in a microwave-safe bowl and microwave in 30-second increments until melted.

2. In a medium bowl, whisk the milk and pudding mix until thickened and smooth. Let set for 5 minutes.

3. Line the bottom of the pan with half of the cookies. Drizzle with one-third of the melted peanut butter. Evenly spread half of the pudding over the cookies and peanut butter. Top with half of the whipped topping. Sprinkle with half of the chopped peanut butter cups.

4. Repeat the layers with the remaining cookies, one-third of the melted peanut butter, and the remaining pudding and whipped topping.

5. Decorate the top of the cake with the remaining melted peanut butter, chopped peanut butter cups, and some crushed cookies. Drizzle hot fudge sauce and caramel sauce over the top.

6. Cover and refrigerate for 8 hours. Scoop and serve.

Boston Cream Pie

Yield: Serves 10 to 12 | Prep Time: 50 minutes, plus 1 hour chill time | Cook Time: 25 to 30 minutes

Cakes and pies used to be baked in the same pan, which is why this dish is called a "pie" even though it's a cake. The first known version of Boston cream pie was made in the 1850s, and in 1996, it became the official state dessert of Massachusetts.

INGREDIENTS

Chocolate Ganache Glaze

1 cup heavy cream

8 ounces bittersweet dark chocolate, chopped

1 teaspoon vanilla bean paste or vanilla extract

Cake

1 (15.25-ounce) box yellow cake mix

Vegetable oil as needed for the cake mix

Eggs as needed for the cake mix

Filling

1 cup milk

1 (3.4-ounce) box vanilla instant pudding mix

1½ cups frozen whipped topping, thawed

1 teaspoon rum extract

DIRECTIONS

1. *For the chocolate ganache glaze:* Heat the cream in the microwave or on the stovetop just until simmering. Place the chocolate in a heatproof bowl, pour the hot cream over the chocolate, and let stand for 2 to 3 minutes, then stir until smooth. Whisk in the vanilla. Let the glaze cool and set at room temperature, about 30 minutes.

2. *For the cake:* Preheat the oven and grease two 9-inch round cake pans. Make the yellow cake according to the package directions. Let the cakes cool in the pans for 10 minutes, then turn out onto a wire rack and let cool completely.

3. *For the filling:* In a medium bowl, whisk the milk and pudding mix until thickened and smooth. Gently fold in the whipped topping and rum extract. Let stand for 5 minutes.

4. Place 1 cake layer on a serving plate, spread the filling evenly over the cake, and then place the other cake layer on top. Whisk the ganache glaze again, then spread on the top of the cake and let the glaze drip down the sides of the cake.

5. Refrigerate for at least 1 hour before slicing and serving.

Homemade Strawberry Shortcakes

Yield: Serves 12 | Prep Time: 15 to 20 minutes | Cook Time: 12 to 15 minutes

When I have a group of friends over during the summer, I have so much fun serving up strawberry shortcakes. When you have different elements on the table, like the biscuits, whipped topping, and strawberries, your food becomes an activity as well as something to nibble on, which winds up being a huge hit at parties. They allow everyone to have their own individual serving of cake, prepared just for them!

INGREDIENTS

1 pound fresh strawberries, hulled and sliced

¼ cup plus 2 tablespoons granulated sugar

¾ cup heavy cream

1 large egg

2½ cups all-purpose flour

1 tablespoon baking powder

½ teaspoon kosher salt

10 tablespoons (1¼ sticks) unsalted butter, cut into cubes, cold

Coarse sugar for sprinkling

1 cup heavy cream

¼ cup confectioners' sugar

1 teaspoon vanilla bean paste or vanilla extract

DIRECTIONS

1. Preheat the oven to 425°F. Line a rimmed 10 × 14½-inch baking sheet with parchment paper.

2. In a medium bowl, mix the strawberries with 2 tablespoons of the granulated sugar and let sit.

3. In a measuring cup, whisk together the cream and egg. In a medium bowl, whisk together the flour, the remaining ¼ cup granulated sugar, the baking powder, and salt. Add the butter cubes to the flour mixture and, using a pastry cutter or 2 forks, cut in until you have coarse crumbs. Add the cream mixture and stir until the dough comes together.

4. Turn the dough out onto a floured work surface and pat out about 1 inch thick. Fold the dough into thirds. Pat out again to 1 inch thick. Using a 2-inch biscuit cutter, cut out 12 biscuits. Place them on the baking sheet and sprinkle coarse sugar over the tops.

5. Bake for 12 to 15 minutes until the tops are golden brown. Place on a wire rack to cool.

6. Using a hand mixer or a stand mixer with a chilled bowl and whisk attachment, whip the cream, confectioners' sugar, and vanilla on low speed for a few minutes, then increase the speed to high and whip until soft, medium peaks form.

7. Split the biscuits and place the bottoms on dessert plates. Top with whipped cream and strawberries. Set the biscuit tops in place and add more whipped cream and strawberries as desired. Serve.

Buttermilk Spice Layer Cake

Yield: Serves 8 to 10 | Prep Time: 15 minutes | Cook Time: 25 to 30 minutes

This old-fashioned layer cake is something I like to save for special occasions. The combination of ginger, cinnamon, nutmeg, and allspice creates a fall-like flavor that becomes extra-creamy and comforting when you combine it with the buttermilk.

INGREDIENTS

2½ cups all-purpose flour, plus extra for the pans

2 cups packed light brown sugar

16 tablespoons (2 sticks) unsalted butter, softened

2 teaspoons vanilla bean paste or vanilla extract

3 large eggs, room temperature

¼ cup cornstarch

4 teaspoons baking powder

2 teaspoons ground ginger

1½ teaspoons ground cinnamon

½ teaspoon ground nutmeg

½ teaspoon ground allspice

½ teaspoon salt

1 cup buttermilk, room temperature

2 (12-ounce) containers cream cheese frosting

Sliced almonds for topping

DIRECTIONS

1. Preheat the oven to 350°F. Lightly grease and flour four 8-inch round cake pans. Line the pans with parchment paper.

2. Using a hand mixer or a stand mixer fitted with the paddle attachment, beat the brown sugar and butter on medium speed until light and fluffy. Beat in the vanilla and then the eggs, one at a time. In a medium bowl, combine the flour, cornstarch, baking powder, ginger, cinnamon, nutmeg, allspice, and salt.

3. On low speed, add the flour mixture to the butter mixture in 3 batches, alternating with the buttermilk in 2 batches, beating until combined. Divide the batter between the cake pans. Bake for 25 to 30 minutes or until the cake is golden brown and a toothpick inserted in the center comes out clean. Let the cakes cool in the pans for 10 minutes, then turn out onto a wire rack, remove the parchment, and let cool completely.

4. Place 1 cake layer on a serving plate and spread some of the frosting over it. Stack the remaining layers on top, frosting each one, then frost the top and sides of the cake. Top with sliced almonds. Slice and serve.

Ultimate Cookie Layer Cake

Yield: Serves 8 to 10 | Prep Time: 15 minutes | Cook Time: 45 minutes

Birthday cakes should have that little something extra. With colorful sprinkles and the combination of both cake and cookie, this is a dessert that'll surely impress your guests—including the guest of honor!

INGREDIENTS

Chocolate Chip Cookie Layer

12 tablespoons (1½ sticks) salted butter, softened

¾ cup packed dark brown sugar

¼ cup granulated sugar

1 large egg

2 teaspoons vanilla bean paste or vanilla extract

2 cups all-purpose flour

2 teaspoons cornstarch

1 teaspoon baking soda

1¼ cups semisweet chocolate chips

Funfetti Layers

1 (15.25-ounce) box Funfetti cake mix

Vegetable oil as needed for the cake mix

Eggs as needed for the cake mix

2 tablespoons hot fudge sauce

2 (16-ounce) cans vanilla frosting

DIRECTIONS

1. Preheat the oven to 350°F. Line three 9-inch round cake pans with parchment paper and grease the sides.

2. *For the chocolate chip cookie layer:* Using a stand mixer fitted with the paddle attachment, beat the butter with the brown sugar and granulated sugar for 3 to 4 minutes on medium speed or until light and fluffy. Beat in the egg and vanilla. Add the flour, cornstarch, and baking soda and beat until well combined. Stir in the chocolate chips. Press the dough into an even layer in the bottom of one of the cake pans. Set aside.

3. *For the Funfetti layers:* Make the Funfetti cake according to the package directions. Pour half of the batter into a cake pan. Mix the hot fudge sauce with the remaining batter and pour into the remaining cake pan.

4. Bake the cookie layer for 18 to 20 minutes or until the edges are slightly golden, and bake the Funfetti layers according to the package directions. Let the layers cool in the pans until just warm. Turn the layers out onto a wire rack, remove the parchment, and let cool completely.

5. Set the cookie layer on a serving plate and spread some of the frosting over the top. Set the white Funfetti layer on top and spread more frosting over the cake, then top it with the chocolate Funfetti layer and spread more frosting on top. Decorate with sprinkles. Slice and serve.

Birthday Funfetti Layer Cake

Yield: Serves 8 to 10　|　Prep Time: 15 minutes　|　Cook Time: 33 to 37 minutes

When you need a more elegant birthday treat than the ultradecadent Ultimate Chocolate Chip Cookie Layer Cake (page 198), this pristine yet colorful Funfetti cake has your name written all over it. The addition of Greek yogurt gives it a lush, moist texture, which will surely have guests asking for seconds.

INGREDIENTS

Cake

3⅓ cups all-purpose flour

1 teaspoon baking powder

½ teaspoon baking soda

1 teaspoon salt

16 tablespoons (2 sticks) unsalted butter, melted

1½ cup granulated sugar

½ cup packed light brown sugar

1½ cups milk

½ cup plain Greek yogurt

2 large eggs

2 tablespoons vanilla bean paste or vanilla extract

1⅓ cup rainbow sprinkles

Vanilla Buttercream Frosting

16 tablespoons (2 sticks) unsalted butter, softened

3–4 cups confectioners' sugar

¼ cup heavy cream

2 teaspoons vanilla bean paste or vanilla extract

Rainbow sprinkles for decorating

DIRECTIONS

1. *For the cake:* Preheat the oven to 350°F. Grease three 9-inch springform or baking pans (round or square). In a medium bowl, whisk together the flour, baking powder, baking soda, and salt. In a large bowl, vigorously whisk the melted butter, granulated sugar, and brown sugar until the mixture is lump-free. Whisk in the milk, yogurt, egg, and vanilla until combined. Slowly add the flour mixture and mix until no lumps remain. The batter will be thick. Stir in the sprinkles just until incorporated (do not overmix because the sprinkles will bleed their color).

2. Pour the batter into the pans. Bake for 20 minutes, then cover loosely with aluminum foil and continue baking for 13 to 17 minutes or until a toothpick inserted in the center comes out clean. Let the cakes cool in the pan for 10 minutes. Remove from the pan and let cool completely on a wire rack.

3. *For the vanilla buttercream frosting:* Using a hand mixer or a stand mixer fitted with the paddle attachment, beat the butter on medium speed for 3 minutes, until smooth and creamy. On low speed, add 3 cups of the confectioners' sugar, the cream, and the vanilla. Increase the speed to high and beat for 3 minutes. Add more confectioners' sugar if the frosting is too thin. Place the cake on a serving plate and frost the top and sides. Decorate with sprinkles. Slice and serve.

Loaded Chocolate Chip Cookie Cake

Yield: Serves 8 to 10 | Prep Time: 20 minutes | Cook Time: 25 to 35 minutes

When it comes to party desserts, there are two camps: those who prefer cake and those who prefer cookie cake. If you're hosting a party, I recommend making both a conventional cake and this candy-filled cookie cake—you're sure to win everyone's favor.

INGREDIENTS

2 cups all-purpose flour

2 teaspoons baking powder

12 tablespoons (1½ sticks) unsalted butter

¾ cup packed light brown sugar

¼ cup granulated sugar

1 large egg plus 1 large egg yolk, room temperature

1 tablespoon vanilla bean paste or vanilla extract

¾ cup chopped peanut butter cups

½ cup white chocolate chips

½ cup M&M'S

DIRECTIONS

1. Preheat the oven to 350°F. Grease a 9-inch pie dish or round cake pan.

2. In a medium bowl, combine the flour and baking powder. Set aside.

3. Using a hand mixer or a stand mixer fitted with the paddle attachment, beat the butter on medium speed for 2 minutes or until completely smooth and creamy. Add the brown sugar and granulated sugar and beat until creamy, about 1 minute. Beat in the egg, egg yolk, and vanilla on medium speed until just combined. Stop the mixer; scrape down the sides and bottom of the bowl. On low speed, add in the flour mixture until just combined. Using a rubber spatula, fold in ½ cup of the chopped peanut butter cups along with most of the white chocolate chips and M&M'S (reserving about 2 tablespoons of each for the topping).

4. Press the cookie dough evenly into the pie dish. Sprinkle the remaining ¼ cup chopped peanut butter cups and remaining white chocolate chips and M&M'S over the dough. Bake for 25 to 35 minutes or until the cake is lightly golden brown. (If necessary, cover the cake loosely with aluminum foil after the first 15 minutes of baking to avoid excess browning.) Transfer the pie dish to a wire rack and let the cookie cake cool completely. Slice and serve.

Baby Shower Cake

Yield: Serves 8 to 10 | Prep Time: 20 minutes | Cook Time: 25 to 35 minutes

You don't need to run out to the bakery and order a fancy, specialized cake in order to have something fun and inventive. Using just cake mix and frosting in a can, you can create an affordable yet adorable themed cake. I made this for a baby shower, but there are other shapes you can make—be creative! I recommend testing out making the shapes with a piece of paper first so you feel confident when you have the cake in front of you.

INGREDIENTS

1 (15.25-ounce) box white cake mix

Vegetable oil as needed for the cake mix

Egg whites as needed for the cake mix

2 (12-ounce) containers buttercream frosting

Sprinkles for decorating

DIRECTIONS

1. Preheat the oven and make the white cake according to the package directions, using a 9 × 13-inch baking dish. Let cool completely. Trim the top of the cake flat and invert it onto a serving platter.

2. Cut a half circle from the middle of one of the short ends of the cake. This will be the onesie's neck hole. Cut rounded corners off the opposite end of the cake to make the onesie's leg holes.

3. Discard (or nibble on) the neck cut-out, but save the leg cut-outs to make the onesie's sleeves. Trim the edge of the cut-outs so they're flat. Place the cut edges against the sides of the cake, lining the corners up with the top edge of the cake. You now have your onesie's shape!

4. Spread frosting evenly over the top and sides of the cake and decorate with sprinkles. Place any remaining frosting in a pastry bag fitted with a small round tip and outline the edges to clearly define the onesie's shape. Slice and serve.

Bouquet of Roses Cake

Yield: Serves 10 to 12 | Prep Time: 20 minutes | Cook Time: 25 to 30 minutes

Ombré cakes, cakes that show a gradient of a single color, are an elegant way to show off your trendy skills in the kitchen. This version incorporates my favorite shades of pink, like a huge bouquet of roses, giving the cake a sweet yet classy look.

INGREDIENTS

3 cups all-purpose flour, plus extra for the pans

16 tablespoons (2 sticks) unsalted butter, softened

½ cup vegetable shortening

3 cups sugar

5 large eggs

2 teaspoons baking powder

¼ teaspoon salt

½ cup milk, room temperature

½ cup buttermilk, room temperature

2 teaspoons vanilla bean paste or vanilla extract

Red liquid food coloring

2 (16-ounce) containers vanilla frosting

DIRECTIONS

1. Preheat the oven to 350°F. Grease and flour four 9-inch round cake pans. Line the pans with parchment paper.

2. Using a hand mixer or a stand mixer fitted with the paddle attachment beat the butter and shortening on medium speed until light and fluffy. Slowly add the sugar 1 cup at a time, making sure to fully incorporate each cup before adding another. Beat in the eggs one at a time, incorporating fully.

3. In a separate bowl, sift together the flour, baking powder, and salt. Pour the milk, buttermilk, and vanilla into a measuring cup and whisk together with a fork. On low speed, add the flour mixture to the butter mixture in 3 batches, alternating with the milk mixture in 2 batches, beating until combined. Scrape down the sides and bottom of the bowl as necessary.

4. Divide the batter evenly into 4 bowls. Add 2 drops food coloring to one, 4 drops food coloring to the second, 6 drops to the third, and 8 drops to the fourth, or to your desired shades of pink, and stir until the coloring is incorporated. Pour each bowl of batter into a cake pan. Bake for 25 to 30 minutes or until a toothpick inserted in the center comes out clean. Let the cakes cool in the pans for 10 minutes, then turn out onto a wire rack and let cool completely.

5. Place the dark pink cake layer on a serving plate and spread a thin layer of frosting over it. Repeat with the remaining layers, getting lighter as you go, and spread the remaining frosting on the top and sides of the cake. Slice and serve.

Rice Krispies Cake

Yield: Serves 8–10 | Prep Time: 30 minutes | Cook Time: 2 minutes

With a little one at home, I'm always brainstorming new treats I can make for him when he's old enough. I think a cake like this would be a hit at a kid's birthday party, especially because he could help me make it!

INGREDIENTS

6 tablespoons butter

2 (10.5-ounce) packages miniature marshmallows

12 cups Rice Krispies cereal

¾ cup multi-colored sprinkles

Red food coloring

1 (15.6-ounce) container vanilla frosting

DIRECTIONS

1. Spray three 8-inch round pans with cooking spray.

2. Microwave the butter in a large microwaveable bowl on high for 45 seconds, or until melted.

3. Add the marshmallows and toss to coat.

4. Stirring halfway through, microwave on high for 90 seconds or until the marshmallows are completely melted and the mixture is well blended.

5. Add the Rice Krispies cereal and ½ cup of the sprinkles and mix well.

6. Divide into three batches and press evenly into the bottoms of the pans. Cool completely.

7. Remove the cereal mixtures from the pans. Add 10 drops of red food coloring to the frosting and mix to combine. Place one on a cake pan and spread ⅓ of the frosting on top. Repeat with the remaining two layers. Add the remaining ¼ cup of sprinkles on top. Slice and serve.

Carrot Cake Roll

Yield: Serves 12 | Prep Time: 20 minutes plus 2 hours chill time | Cook Time: 10 to 15 minutes

Carrot cake is a springtime favorite, and when presented as a cake roll, this old-fashioned dessert seems fresh and new again.

INGREDIENTS

Cake

3 large eggs

⅔ cup granulated sugar

2 tablespoons vegetable oil

1 teaspoon vanilla bean paste or vanilla extract

¾ cup all-purpose flour

2 teaspoons ground cinnamon

1½ teaspoons minced crystallized ginger

1 teaspoon baking powder

½ teaspoon kosher salt

¼ teaspoon ground nutmeg

¼ teaspoon ground allspice

4 carrots, peeled and shredded (2 cups)

Filling

6 ounces cream cheese, room temperature

4 tablespoons unsalted butter, softened

2 cups confectioners' sugar, plus extra for dusting

1 teaspoon vanilla bean paste or vanilla extract

DIRECTIONS

1. *For the cake:* Preheat the oven to 350°F. Lightly spray a 10 × 15-inch jelly-roll pan with cooking spray. Line the pan with parchment paper, leaving a 1-inch overhang on the short sides of the pan. Lightly spray the parchment paper.

2. Using a hand mixer or a stand mixer fitted with the whisk attachment, beat the eggs on high speed for 5 minutes until thick and foamy. Beat in the sugar, oil, and vanilla until incorporated.

3. In a small bowl, whisk together the flour, cinnamon, ginger, baking powder, salt, nutmeg, and allspice. Stir into the wet ingredients. Fold in the carrots until incorporated.

4. Spread the batter into the pan; it will be a very thin batter. Bake for 10 to 15 minutes or until set. (Do not underbake the cake, or you will not be able to roll it.)

5. Let the cake cool in the pan for 5 minutes. Use the parchment paper to lift the cake out of the pan and place on a flat surface. Using the parchment paper, roll the cake up tightly, starting at the short end. Do not press too hard. Let the cake cool completely, for 1 hour.

6. *For the filling:* Using a hand mixer or a stand mixer fitted with the paddle attachment, beat the cream cheese and butter until smooth. Beat in the confectioners' sugar and vanilla bean paste. On a flat surface, carefully unroll the cake. Spread the filling evenly on the cake. Reroll the cake, removing the parchment as you go.

7. Place the cake on a serving platter. Refrigerate 1 hour or until firm.

8. Dust the top of the cake with confectioners' sugar. Slice and serve.

Mardi Gras King Cake

Yield: Serves 12 | Prep Time: 30 minutes plus 2 hours rising time | Cook Time: 20 to 35 minutes

Mardi Gras is cause for celebration and festivities, and when you see the variety of colors on this cake, you can't help but smile and join in on the fun.

INGREDIENTS

Cake

1 cup milk

¼ cup granulated sugar

1 teaspoon kosher salt

3½ cups all-purpose flour

1 (0.25-ounce) package quick-rise yeast

2 large eggs

6 tablespoons unsalted butter, cut into 12 slices, softened

Filling

⅔ cup packed light brown sugar

1½ teaspoons ground cinnamon

4 tablespoons unsalted butter, softened

Glaze

1 cup confectioners' sugar

1 tablespoon milk or heavy cream

½ teaspoon vanilla bean paste or vanilla extract

Green, purple, and yellow/gold sugar sprinkles for decorating

DIRECTIONS

1. *For the cake:* Heat the milk, sugar, and salt in a small saucepan over medium heat until the milk is 120°F.

2. Mix 2½ cups of the flour with the yeast for 30 seconds on medium until combined. Reduce to low, pour in the milk mixture, and blend in. Add the eggs. Mix until a shaggy dough forms. Switch to the dough hook. On low speed, add the remaining 1 cup of flour gradually to form a soft dough, then add the butter slices one at a time and knead until incorporated. Continue kneading for about 8 minutes.

3. Turn the dough onto a lightly floured surface. Knead a few times by hand until smooth. Shape into a smooth ball and place in a greased bowl. Cover with plastic wrap and refrigerate for 1 hour.

4. *For the filling:* In a small bowl, mix the brown sugar with the cinnamon. Add the butter and whisk until blended in.

5. Roll the dough into a 10 × 20-inch rectangle. Spread the filling over the dough, then roll up the rectangle jelly-roll style, starting at the long end. Place the roll on a parchment paper–lined baking sheet. Bring the ends together to form an oval ring. Pinch the ends together to seal. Cover with plastic wrap and let rise for an hour.

6. While the cake is rising, preheat the oven to 350°F. Bake for 20 to 35 minutes or until golden. Transfer to a wire rack and cool completely.

7. *For the glaze:* In a small bowl, whisk the confectioners' sugar, milk, and vanilla until smooth. Drizzle the glaze over the cake. Sprinkle the colored sugars over the glaze, alternating the colors. Slice and serve.

Firecracker Cake

Yield: Serves 8 to 10 | Prep Time: 15 minutes | Cook Time: 45 minutes

The Fourth of July needs to have a couple of dishes that "go off with a bang," and this red, white, and blue Firecracker Cake certainly fits the bill. With explosions of color, this cake is a memorable and patriotic treat.

INGREDIENTS

Cake

Flour for the pan

1 (15.25-ounce) box white cake mix

Vegetable oil as needed for the cake mix

Egg whites as needed for the cake mix

Red liquid food coloring

Blue liquid food coloring

Glaze

1½ cups confectioners' sugar, sifted to remove any lumps

3–4 tablespoons milk or water

2 teaspoons vanilla bean paste or vanilla extract

Blue liquid food coloring

DIRECTIONS

1. *For the cake:* Preheat the oven according to the cake mix package directions. Grease and flour a 12-cup Bundt pan; set aside.

2. Prepare the white cake batter according to the package directions. Divide the batter equally into 3 parts. Add 6 drops red food coloring to one and 6 drops blue food coloring to another.

3. Pour the blue cake batter into the Bundt pan. Carefully pour the white batter over the blue batter and pour the red batter over the white batter. Swirl with a knife.

4. Bake according to the package directions or until a toothpick inserted in the center comes out clean. Let the cake cool in the pan for 10 minutes. Place a wire rack over a baking sheet. Invert the pan onto the rack. Let the cake cool completely, 30 to 45 minutes.

5. *For the glaze:* Whisk together the confectioners' sugar, milk, and vanilla. Stir in a few drops of the blue food coloring until well blended. Drizzle over the cake, scattering back and forth. Let the cake stand at room temperature until the glaze is set. Slice and serve.

Gingerbread Cake

Yield: Serves 12 | Prep Time: 20 minutes | Cook Time: 30 to 35 minutes

Christmas is the perfect time to pull out all of your favorite dessert recipes and share the spoils with your neighbors, coworkers, dog walker, and more. This gingerbread cake is a festive way to share the tastes of the season.

INGREDIENTS

Cake

3 (14.5-ounce) boxes gingerbread cake mix

Vegetable oil as needed for the cake mix

Eggs as needed for the cake mix

Frosting

1 cup heavy cream

2 cups confectioners' sugar

12 ounces cream cheese, room temperature

½ teaspoon vanilla bean paste or vanilla extract

DIRECTIONS

1. *For the cake:* Preheat the oven and make the gingerbread cake according to the package directions, using three 8-inch round cake pans (one for each box of cake mix).

2. Let the cakes cool in the pans for 10 minutes, then turn out onto a wire rack and let cool completely.

3. *For the frosting:* Using a hand mixer or a stand mixer with a chilled bowl and whisk attachment, beat the cream and confectioners' sugar until medium peaks form. Transfer to a medium bowl. Place the cream cheese and vanilla in the empty mixer bowl and whip until smooth. Gradually add the whipped cream to the cream cheese mixture and whip just until combined.

4. Place 1 cake layer on a serving plate. Spread a generous amount of the frosting over the top, then set another cake layer in place and repeat. Add the last layer and frost the top and sides of the cake. Slice and serve.

NOTES

Each cake mix makes one 8-inch cake. You can use your favorite gingerbread cake recipe instead of using a box mix.

Christmas Vanilla Cake Roll

Yield: Serves 8 to 10 | Prep Time: 15 minutes plus 2 hours chill time | Cook Time: 6 to 7 minutes

Cake rolls are an ideal sweet to make during the holiday season. They're easier than layer cakes because you don't have to worry about them toppling over or having a layer slide out of place.

INGREDIENTS

Cake

4 large eggs (2 whole, 2 separated) plus 1 large egg yolk

½ cup plus 1 tablespoon granulated sugar

1 teaspoon vanilla bean paste or vanilla extract

⅓ cup sifted cake flour

3 tablespoons cornstarch

¼ cup confectioners' sugar, plus extra for dusting

Vanilla Buttercream

16 tablespoons (2 sticks) unsalted butter, softened

3 cups confectioners' sugar

1 teaspoon vanilla bean paste or vanilla extract

Heavy cream, as needed

Red liquid food coloring

10 regular York Peppermint Patties, chopped

DIRECTIONS

1. *For the cake:* Preheat the oven to 450°F. Line a 17 × 11-inch rimmed baking pan with parchment paper. Set aside.

2. Using a hand mixer or a stand mixer fitted with the paddle attachment, beat the 2 whole eggs, 3 egg yolks, and ½ cup of the sugar on high speed for about 5 minutes or until thickened. Add the vanilla and beat to incorporate.

3. In a small bowl, whisk together the flour and cornstarch. Sift over the egg mixture and gently fold in with a spatula. In a separate bowl, combine the 2 egg whites and the remaining 1 tablespoon sugar. Whisk until firm peaks form. Fold into the egg mixture.

4. Pour the cake batter into the pan, spread it evenly, and bake for 6 to 7 minutes or until golden and springy when touched.

5. As soon as you remove the cake from the oven, dust with ¼ cup confectioners' sugar and then invert onto a clean dish towel. Remove the parchment paper, dust with more confectioners' sugar and roll up the cake on the short side with the towel. Place on a wire rack to cool.

6. *For the vanilla buttercream:* Using a hand mixer or a stand mixer fitted with the whisk attachment, whip the butter on medium speed for 2 to 3 minutes. Reduce the speed to low and slowly add the confectioners' sugar, ½ cup at a time. When incorporated, increase the speed to medium and whip for 2 minutes. Add few drops of cream if needed to create a smooth, spreadable consistency. Add red food coloring to achieve a pink/red color. Add the peppermint patties and mix by hand. Gently unroll the cake and spread the buttercream evenly all over it. Roll it up again, set on a serving platter, and refrigerate for 2 hours. Slice and serve.

Acknowledgments

Thank you to my incredibly creative culinary team at Prime Publishing. To Megan Von Schönhoff and Tom Krawczyk, my photographers. To Chris Hammond and Marlene Stolfo, my test kitchen geniuses. To word masters and editors Bryn Clark and Jessica Thelander. And to my amazing editor and friend, Kara Rota. Thank you to Stuart Hochwert and the entire team at Prime Publishing, for their enthusiasm and support. Thank you to Will Schwalbe, Erica Martirano, Justine Sha, Jaclyn Waggner, and the entire staff at St. Martin's Griffin for helping this book come to life. This book was a team effort, filled with collaboration and creativity that reached no limits.

Index

almond(s)
    Hubby's Favorite Dump Cake, 127
    Old-Fashioned Fruitcake, 69
Amish Applesauce Cake, 83
Angel Cake, Creamy Lemon, 65
angel food cake
    The Best Angel Food Cake, 62
    Blueberry Angel Food Sheet Cake, 107
    Heaven and Hell Cake, 108
    Key Lime Angel Food Cake, 185
    Pumpkin Angel Food Cake, 182
apple(s)
    Amish Applesauce Cake, 83
    Apple Pie Dump Cake with Pecan
        Topping, 124
    Cinnamon Apple Crumb Cake, 7
    Cinnamon Cream Cheese Apple
        Cake, 115
apricot(s)
    Old-Fashioned Fruitcake, 69

Baby Shower Cake, 205
Banana Pudding Poke Cake, 147
berry(ies)
    Almond Honey Cake, 99
    The Best Angel Food Cake, 62
    Blueberry Angel Food Sheet Cake, 107
    Buttermilk Blueberry Coffee Cake, 11
    Cranberry-Pecan Coffee Cake, 12
    Homemade Strawberry
        Shortcakes, 194
    Lemon Shortcake Icebox Cake, 73
    Moist Vanilla Mug Cake, 156
    No-Bake Strawberry Icebox Cake, 74
    Old-Fashioned Fruitcake, 69
    Slow Cooker Chocolate Lava
        Cake, 136
    Strawberry Jell-O Poke Cake, 144
    Strawberry-Chocolate Mousse
        Cake, 173
    Victoria Sponge Cake, 66

The Best Angel Food Cake, 62
The Best Pumpkin Mug Cake, 163
Best-Ever German Chocolate Cake, 91
Birthday Funfetti Layer Cake, 201
Black Forest Cake, 174
Blueberry Angel Food Sheet Cake, 107
blueberry(ies)
    Almond Honey Cake, 99
    Blueberry Angel Food Sheet
        Cake, 107
    Buttermilk Blueberry Coffee
        Cake, 11
Boston Cream Pie, 193
Bouquet of Roses Cake, 206
brandy
    Old-Fashioned Fruitcake, 69
Brownie Butter Cake, 37
bundt cakes
    Brownie Butter Cake, 37
    Cream Cheese Red Velvet Cake, 26
    Lime Bundt Cake, 21
    Pink Lemonade Bundt Cake, 30
    Samoa Bundt Cake, 22
butter cakes
    Brownie Butter Cake, 37
    Gooiest Butter Cake, 177
    Kentucky Butter Cake, 18
buttermilk
    Bouquet of Roses Cake, 206
    Buttermilk Blueberry Coffee
        Cake, 11
    Buttermilk Spice Layer Cake, 197
    Chocolate Pound Cake, 45
    Classic Chocolate Cake, 119
    Coconut Pound Cake, 41
    Cream Cheese Red Velvet Cake, 26
    Italian Lemon Mini Pound Cakes, 38
    Kentucky Butter Cake, 18
    Mint Patty Cake, 112
    Moist Fluffy Coconut Cake, 104
    Pecan Pie Coffee Cake, 15
    Pineapple Upside-Down Cake, 61

Cake Roll, Cinnamon Roll, 96
Cannoli Poke Cake, 148
caramel
    Amish Applesauce Cake, 83
    Apple Pie Dump Cake with Pecan
        Topping, 124
    Carrot Cake Poke Cake, 151
    Chocolate Turtle Poke Cake, 140
    Grandmother's Lazy Daisy Cake, 57
    Peanut Butter Lover's Icebox
        Cake, 190
    Snickers Poke Cake, 132
    Southern Caramel Cake, 170
carrot cakes
    Carrot Cake Poke Cake, 151
    Carrot Cake Roll, 210
cheese
    Buttermilk Spice Layer Cake, 197
    Cannoli Poke Cake, 148
    Carrot Cake Roll, 210
    Church Cake, 88
    Cinnamon Cream Cheese Apple
        Cake, 115
    Cinnamon Roll Cake Roll, 96
    Cinnamon Roll Pound Cake, 34
    Dandy Diner Dream Cake, 58
    Dreamsicle Cake, 169
    Gingerbread Cake, 217
    Gooiest Butter Cake, 177
    Heaven and Hell Cake, 108
    Inside-Out Cream Puff Cake, 95
    Italian Lemon Mini Pound
        Cakes, 38
    Italian Love Cake, 111
    Lemon Shortcake Icebox Cake, 73
    Millionaire Marshmallow Fluff
        Cake, 103
    Moist, Fluffy Coconut Cake, 104
    No-Bake Strawberry Icebox Cake, 74
    Oreo Icebox Dessert, 189
    Pecan Pie Coffee Cake, 15
    Refrigerator Fudge Cake, 70

cherry(ies)
  Black Forest Cake, 174
  Cherry 7UP Pound Cake, 46
  Cherry Coffee Cake, 8
  Dandy Diner Dream Cake, 58
  Hubby's Favorite Dump Cake, 127
  Old-Fashioned Fruitcake, 69
  Piña Colada Dump Cake, 131
  Pineapple Upside-Down Cake, 61
chocolate
  Best-Ever German Chocolate Cake, 91
  Black Forest Cake, 174
  Boston Cream Pie, 193
  Brownie Butter Cake, 37
  Cannoli Poke Cake, 148
  Chocolate Oreo Cake, 178
  Chocolate Pound Cake, 45
  Chocolate Turtle Poke Cake, 140
  Classic Chocolate Cake, 119
  Classic Texas Sheet Cake, 80
  Cookies 'n' Cream Mug Cake, 159
  Dandy Diner Dream Cake, 58
  Fudgy S'mores Mug Cake, 160
  Grandma's Famous Jimmy Cake, 50
  Heaven and Hell Cake, 108
  Hot Chocolate Cake, 186
  Inside-Out Cream Puff Cake, 95
  Italian Love Cake, 111
  Loaded Chocolate Chip Cookie
    Cake, 202
  No-Bake Chocolate Éclair Cake, 120
  No-Bake Strawberry Icebox Cake, 74
  Oreo Icebox Dessert, 189
  Peanut Butter Cup Cake, 181
  Peanut Butter Lover's Icebox Cake, 190
  Refrigerator Fudge Cake, 70
  Samoa Bundt Cake, 22
  Slow Cooker Chocolate Lava Cake,
    136
  Snickers Poke Cake, 132
  Strawberry-Chocolate Mousse Cake,
    173
  Ultimate Cookie Layer Cake, 198
Chocolate Chip Cookie Cake,
    Loaded, 202
Christmas Vanilla Cake Roll, 218
Church Cake, 88
cinnamon
  Amish Applesauce Cake, 83
  Apple Pie Dump Cake with Pecan
    Topping, 124
  Buttermilk Spice Layer Cake, 197

Cannoli Poke Cake, 148
Carrot Cake Roll, 210
Cinnamon Apple Crumb Cake, 7
Cinnamon Cream Cheese Apple
    Cake, 115
Cinnamon Roll Cake Roll, 96
Cinnamon Roll Pound Cake, 34
Cranberry-Pecan Coffee Cake, 12
Fall Pumpkin Dump Cake, 135
Grandmother's Lazy Daisy Cake, 57
Mardi Gras King Cake, 213
Millionaire Marshmallow Fluff
    Cake, 103
Old-Fashioned Fruitcake, 69
Peach Pound Cake, 25
Pumpkin Angel Food Cake, 182
Snickerdoodle Mug Cake, 152
Sour Cream Coffee Cake, 4
Classic Buttery Pound Cake, 33
Classic Chocolate Cake, 119
Classic Texas Sheet Cake, 80
cocoa powder
  Best-Ever German Chocolate Cake, 91
  Chocolate Oreo Cake, 178
  Classic Chocolate Cake, 119
  Classic Texas Sheet Cake, 80
  Fudgy S'mores Mug Cake, 160
  Mint Patty Cake, 112
  Strawberry-Chocolate Mousse Cake,
    173
coconut(s)
  Best-Ever German Chocolate Cake, 91
  Church Cake, 88
  Coconut Pound Cake, 41
  Grandmother's Lazy Daisy Cake, 57
  Millionaire Marshmallow Fluff
    Cake, 103
  Moist, Fluffy Coconut Cake, 104
  Piña Colada Dump Cake, 131
  Samoa Bundt Cake, 22
  Texas Tornado Cake, 92
coffee. See also Espresso powder
  Grandma's Famous Jimmy Cake, 50
coffee cakes
  Buttermilk Blueberry Coffee Cake, 11
  Cherry Coffee Cake, 8
  Cinnamon Apple Crumb Cake, 7
  Cranberry-Pecan Coffee Cake, 12
  Pecan Pie Coffee Cake, 15
  Sour Cream Coffee Cake, 4
Cookie Cake, Loaded Chocolate
    Chip, 202

Cookie Layer Cake, Ultimate, 198
Cookies 'n' Cream Mug Cake, 159
cranberry(ies)
  Cranberry-Pecan Coffee Cake, 12
  Old-Fashioned Fruitcake, 69
Crazy Cake, Lemon, 54
cream cheese
  Buttermilk Spice Layer Cake, 197
  Carrot Cake Roll, 210
  Church Cake, 88
  Cinnamon Cream Cheese Apple
    Cake, 115
  Cinnamon Roll Cake Roll, 96
  Cinnamon Roll Pound Cake, 34
  Cream Cheese Red Velvet Cake, 26
  Dandy Diner Dream Cake, 58
  Dreamsicle Cake, 169
  Gingerbread Cake, 217
  Gooiest Butter Cake, 177
  Heaven and Hell Cake, 108
  Inside-Out Cream Puff Cake, 95
  Millionaire Marshmallow Fluff
    Cake, 103
  Moist, Fluffy Coconut Cake, 104
  Oreo Icebox Dessert, 189
  Pecan Pie Coffee Cake, 15
  Refrigerator Fudge Cake, 70
Cream Pie, Boston, 193
Cream Puff Cake, Inside-Out, 95
Creamy Lemon Angel Cake, 65
currant(s)
  Old-Fashioned Fruitcake, 69

Daisy Cake, Grandmother's Lazy, 57
Dandy Diner Dream Cake, 58
devil's food cake mix
  Heaven and Hell Cake, 108
  Oreo Pudding Poke Cake, 143
  Snickers Poke Cake, 132
Dream Cake, Dandy Diner, 58
Dreamsicle Cake, 169
dulce de leche
  Slow Cooker Vanilla-Caramel Poke
    Cake, 139
dump cakes
  Apple Pie Dump Cake with Pecan
    Topping, 124
  Fall Pumpkin Dump Cake, 135
  Funfetti Dump Cake, 128
  Hubby's Favorite Dump Cake, 127
  Piña Colada Dump Cake, 131

espresso powder
  Brownie Butter Cake, 37
  Chocolate Pound Cake, 45
  Classic Chocolate Cake, 119
  Classic Texas Sheet Cake, 80
  Grandma's Famous Jimmy Cake, 50
  Italian Love Cake, 111
  Refrigerator Fudge Cake, 70
  Samoa Bundt Cake, 22
  Slow Cooker Chocolate Lava
    Cake, 136
everyday cakes
  Almond Honey Cake, 99
  Amish Applesauce Cake, 83
  Best-Ever German Chocolate Cake, 91
  Blueberry Angel Food Sheet Cake, 107
  Church Cake, 88
  Cinnamon Cream Cheese Apple
    Cake, 115
  Cinnamon Roll Cake Roll, 96
  Classic Chocolate Cake, 119
  Classic Texas Sheet Cake, 80
  Glazed Rum Cake, 116
  Grandma's Magic Cake, 84
  Heaven and Hell Cake, 108
  Inside-Out Cream Puff Cake, 95
  Italian Love Cake, 111
  Lemon Poppy Seed Cake, 85
  Millionaire Marshmallow Fluff
    Cake, 103
  Mini Patty Cake, 112
  Moist, Fluffy Coconut Cake, 104
  No-Bake Chocolate Éclair Cake, 120
  Texas Tornado Cake, 92
  Zucchini Cake with Browned Butter
    Frosting, 100

Fall Pumpkin Dump Cake, 135
Firecracker Cake, 214
Four-Ingredient Molten Nutella Lava
  Cake, 155
frosting
  Baby Shower Cake, 205
  Best-Ever German Chocolate Cake, 91
  Birthday Funfetti Layer Cake, 201
  Black Forest Cake, 174
  Bouquet of Roses Cake, 206
  Buttermilk Spice Layer Cake, 197
  Chocolate Oreo Cake, 178
  Church Cake, 88
  Classic Chocolate Cake, 119

  Classic Texas Sheet Cake, 80
  Dandy Diner Dream Cake, 58
  Gingerbread Cake, 217
  Grandmother's Lazy Daisy Cake, 57
  Italian Love Cake, 111
  Lemon Chiffon Layer Cake, 166
  Lemon Crazy Cake, 54
  Mint Patty Cake, 112
  Moist, Fluffy Coconut Cake, 104
  Samoa Bundt Cake, 22
  Ultimate Cookie Layer Cake, 198
  Zucchini Cake with Browned Butter
    Frosting, 100
fruit cocktail
  Texas Tornado Cake, 92
Fruitcake, Old-Fashioned, 69
Fudge Cake, Refrigerator, 70
Fudgy S'mores Mug Cake, 160
Funfetti cake mix
  Birthday Funfetti Layer Cake, 201
  Funfetti Dump Cake, 128
  Ultimate Cookie Layer Cake, 198

Galliano liqueur
  1970s Harvey Wallbanger Cake, 53
ganache
  Boston Cream Pie, 193
  Chocolate Pound Cake, 45
  Heaven and Hell Cake, 108
  Hot Chocolate Cake, 186
  Strawberry-Chocolate Mousse
    Cake, 173
German Chocolate Cake, Best-Ever, 91
Gingerbread Cake, 217
Glazed Rum Cake, 116
Gooiest Butter Cake, 177
graham crackers
  Fudgy S'mores Mug Cake, 160
  Millionaire Marshmallow Fluff
    Cake, 103
  No-Bake Chocolate Éclair Cake, 120
Grandma's Famous Jimmy Cake, 50
Grandma's Magic Cake, 84
Grandmother's Lazy Daisy Cake, 57

hazelnut(s)
  Old-Fashioned Fruitcake, 69
Heaven and Hell Cake, 108
holiday cakes. See Special occasion cakes
Homemade Strawberry Shortcakes, 194

Honey Almond Cake, 99
Hot Chocolate Cake, 186
hot fudge sauce
  Neapolitan Bundt Cake, 29
  Peanut Butter Lover's Icebox
    Cake, 190
  Samoa Bundt Cake, 22
  Ultimate Cookie Layer Cake, 198
Hubby's Favorite Dump Cake, 127

icebox cakes
  Lemon Shortcake Icebox Cake, 73
  No-Bake Strawberry Icebox Cake, 74
  Pistachio Icebox Cake, 77
Inside-Out Cream Puff Cake, 95
Italian Lemon Mini Pound Cakes, 38
Italian Love Cake, 111

Jell-O Poke Cake, Strawberry, 144

Kentucky Butter Cake, 18
Key Lime Angel Food Cake, 185
King Cake, Mardi Gras, 213

ladyfingers
  Lemon Shortcake Icebox Cake, 73
  No-Bake Strawberry Icebox Cake, 74
Lava Cake, Four-Ingredient Molten
  Nutella, 155
layer cakes
  Birthday Funfetti Layer Cake, 201
  Buttermilk Spice Layer Cake, 197
  Lemon Chiffon Layer Cake, 166
  Ultimate Chocolate Chip Cookie
    Layer Cake, 198
Lazy Daisy Cake, Grandmother's, 57
lemon(s)
  Cinnamon Cream Cheese Apple
    Cake, 115
  Creamy Lemon Angel Cake, 65
  Grandma's Magic Cake, 84
  Italian Lemon Mini Pound
    Cakes, 38
  Lemon Chiffon Layer Cake, 166
  Lemon Crazy Cake, 54
  Lemon Poppy Seed Cake, 87
  Lemon Shortcake Icebox Cake, 73
  Pink Lemonade Bundt Cake, 30

lime(s)
Coconut Pound Cake, 41
Key Lime Angel Food Cake, 185
Lime Bundt Cake, 21
limoncello liqueur
Italian Lemon Mini Pound Cakes, 38
Loaded Cookie Cake, 202
Love Cake, Italian, 111

M&M'S
Loaded Chocolate Chip Cookie
Cake, 202
Magic Cake, Grandma's, 84
malted milk balls
Classic Chocolate Cake, 119
Mardi Gras King Cake, 213
marshmallows
Fudgy S'mores Mug Cake, 160
Hot Chocolate Cake, 186
Millionaire Marshmallow Fluff
Cake, 103
Rice Krispies Cake, 209
mascarpone cheese
Cannoli Poke Cake, 148
Italian Lemon Mini Pound Cakes, 38
Italian Love Cake, 111
Lemon Shortcake Icebox Cake, 73
No-Bake Strawberry Icebox Cake, 74
Millionaire Marshmallow Fluff
Cake, 103
Mini Patty Cake, 112
Moist, Fluffy Coconut Cake, 104
Moist Vanilla Mug Cake, 156
Mousse Cake, Strawberry-Chocolate, 173
mug cakes
The Best Pumpkin Mug Cake, 163
Cookies 'n' Cream Mug Cake, 159
Fudgy S'mores Mug Cake, 160
Moist Vanilla Mug Cake, 156
Snickerdoodle Mug Cake, 152

Neapolitan Bundt Cake, 29
1970s Harvey Wallbanger Cake, 53
No-Bake Chocolate Éclair Cake, 120
No-Bake Strawberry Icebox Cake, 74
Nutella Lava Cake, Four-Ingredient
Molten, 155

oats
Grandmother's Lazy Daisy Cake, 57

old-fashioned cakes
1970s Harvey Wallbanger Cake, 53
The Best Angel Food Cake, 62
Creamy Lemon Angel Cake, 65
Dandy Diner Dream Cake, 58
Grandma's Famous Jimmy Cake, 50
Grandmother's Lazy Daisy Cake, 57
Lemon Crazy Cake, 54
Lemon Shortcake Icebox Cake, 73
No-Bake Strawberry Icebox Cake, 74
Old-Fashioned Fruitcake, 69
Pineapple Upside-Down Cake, 61
Pistachio Icebox Cake, 77
Refrigerator Fudge Cake, 70
Victoria Sponge Cake, 66
orange(s)
1970s Harvey Wallbanger Cake, 53
The Best Angel Food Cake, 62
Dreamsicle Cake, 169
Old-Fashioned Fruitcake, 69
Victoria Sponge Cake, 66
Oreos
Chocolate Oreo Cake, 178
Funfetti Dump Cake, 128
Oreo Icebox Dessert, 189
Oreo Pudding Poke Cake, 143

Patty Cake, Mint, 112
Peach Pound Cake, 25
peanut butter
Heaven and Hell Cake, 108
Peanut Butter Cup Cake, 181
Peanut Butter Lover's Icebox Cake, 190
peanut(s)
Dandy Diner Dream Cake, 58
Snickers Poke Cake, 132
pecan(s)
Amish Applesauce Cake, 83
Apple Pie Dump Cake with Pecan
Topping, 124
Carrot Cake Poke Cake, 151
Chocolate Turtle Poke Cake, 140
Classic Texas Sheet Cake, 80
Cranberry-Pecan Coffee Cake, 12
Fall Pumpkin Dump Cake, 135
Glazed Rum Cake, 116
Grandmother's Lazy Daisy Cake, 57
Old-Fashioned Fruitcake, 69
Pecan Pie Coffee Cake, 15
Refrigerator Fudge Cake, 70
Southern Caramel Cake, 170
Southern Pecan Pound Cake, 42

Texas Tornado Cake, 92
Zucchini Cake with Browned Butter
Frosting, 100
peppermint patties
Christmas Vanilla Cake Roll, 218
Mint Patty Cake, 112
Piña Colada Dump Cake, 131
pineapple(s)
Church Cake, 88
Hubby's Favorite Dump Cake, 127
Old-Fashioned Fruitcake, 69
Piña Colada Dump Cake, 131
Pineapple Upside-Down Cake, 61
Pink Lemonade Bundt Cake, 30
pistachio(s)
Cannoli Poke Cake, 148
Key Lime Angel Food Cake, 185
Old-Fashioned Fruitcake, 69
Pistachio Icebox Cake, 77
poke cakes
Banana Pudding Poke Cake, 147
Cannoli Poke Cake, 148
Carrot Cake Poke Cake, 151
Chocolate Turtle Poke Cake, 140
Oreo Pudding Poke Cake, 143
Slow Cooker Vanilla-Caramel Poke
Cake, 139
Snickers Poke Cake, 132
Strawberry Jell-O Poke Cake, 144
Poppy Seed Cake, Lemon, 87
pound cakes
Cherry 7UP Pound Cake, 46
Chocolate Pound Cake, 45
Cinnamon Roll Pound Cake, 34
Classic Buttery Pound Cake, 33
Coconut Pound Cake, 41
Italian Lemon Mini Pound
Cakes, 38
Kentucky Butter Cake, 18
Peach Pound Cake, 25
Southern Pecan Pound Cake, 42
pudding mix
1970s Harvey Wallbanger Cake, 53
Banana Pudding Poke Cake, 147
Boston Cream Pie, 193
Carrot Cake Poke Cake, 151
Funfetti Dump Cake, 128
Glazed Rum Cake, 116
Inside-Out Cream Puff Cake, 95
Italian Love Cake, 111
No-Bake Chocolate Éclair Cake, 120
Oreo Icebox Dessert, 189
Oreo Pudding Poke Cake, 143

Peanut Butter Lover's Icebox Cake, 190
Pink Lemonade Bundt Cake, 30
Pistachio Icebox Cake, 77
Slow Cooker Chocolate Lava
 Cake, 136
Slow Cooker Vanilla-Caramel Poke
 Cake, 139
Strawberry Jell-O Poke Cake, 144
Strawberry-Chocolate Mousse
 Cake, 173
pumpkin(s)
 The Best Pumpkin Mug Cake, 163
 Fall Pumpkin Dump Cake, 135
 Pumpkin Angel Food Cake, 182

raisin(s)
 Old-Fashioned Fruitcake, 69
raspberry(ies)
 Almond Honey Cake, 99
 Lemon Shortcake Icebox Cake, 73
 Slow Cooker Chocolate Lava
  Cake, 136
 Victoria Sponge Cake, 66
Refrigerator Fudge Cake, 70
Rice Crispies Cake, 209
ricotta cheese
 Cannoli Poke Cake, 148
 Italian Love Cake, 111
Roses (Bouquet of) Cake, 206
rum
 Banana Pudding Poke Cake, 147
 Boston Cream Pie, 193
 Glazed Rum Cake, 116
 Hubby's Favorite Dump Cake, 127
 Piña Colada Dump Cake, 131
 Pineapple Upside-Down Cake, 61
 Southern Pecan Pound Cake, 42
 Strawberry Jell-O Poke Cake, 144
 Texas Tornado Cake, 92

Samoa Bundt Cake, 22
sandwich cookies
 Cookies 'n' Cream Mug Cake, 159
7UP Pound Cake, Cherry, 46
Sheet Cake, Classic Texas, 80
shortbread cookies
 Pistachio Icebox Cake, 77
shortcakes
 Homemade Strawberry
  Shortcakes, 194
 Shortcake Icebox Cake, Lemon, 73

slow cooker cakes
 Slow Cooker Chocolate Lava
  Cake, 136
 Slow Cooker Vanilla-Caramel Poke
  Cake, 139
S'mores Mug Cake, Fudgy, 160
Snickerdoodle Mug Cake, 152
Snickers Poke Cake, 132
Sour Cream Coffee Cake, 4
Southern Caramel Cake, 170
Southern Pecan Pound Cake, 42
special occasion cakes
 Baby Shower Cake, 205
 Birthday Funfetti Layer Cake, 201
 Black Forest Cake, 174
 Boston Cream Pie, 193
 Bouquet of Roses Cake, 206
 Buttermilk Spice Layer Cake, 197
 Carrot Cake Roll, 210
 Chocolate Oreo Cake, 178
 Christmas Vanilla Cake Roll, 218
 Dreamsicle Cake, 169
 Firecracker Cake, 214
 Gingerbread Cake, 217
 Gooiest Butter Cake, 177
 Homemade Strawberry Shortcake, 194
 Hot Chocolate Cake, 186
 Key Lime Angel Food Cake, 185
 Lemon Chiffon Layer Cake, 166
 Loaded Cookie Cake, 202
 Mardi Gras King Cake, 213
 Oreo Icebox Dessert, 189
 Peanut Butter Cup Cake, 181
 Peanut Butter Lover's Icebox Cake, 190
 Pumpkin Angel Food Cake, 182
 Rice Krispies Cake, 209
 Southern Caramel Cake, 170
 Strawberry-Chocolate Mousse
  Cake, 173
 Ultimate Chocolate Chip Cookie
  Layer Cake, 198
Spice Layer Cake, Buttermilk, 197
Sponge Cake, Victoria, 66
sprinkles
 Baby Shower Cake, 205
 Birthday Funfetti Layer Cake, 201
 Classic Chocolate Cake, 119
 Funfetti Dump Cake, 128
 Grandma's Famous Jimmy Cake, 50
 Mardi Gras King Cake, 213
 Pink Lemonade Bundt Cake, 30
 Rice Krispies Cake, 209
 Ultimate Cookie Layer Cake, 198

strawberry(ies)
 Almond Honey Cake, 99
 Homemade Strawberry
  Shortcakes, 194
 No-Bake Strawberry Icebox
  Cake, 74
 Strawberry Jell-O Poke Cake, 144
 Strawberry-Chocolate Mousse
  Cake, 173
streusel
 Cinnamon Apple Crumb Cake, 7
 Cranberry-Pecan Coffee Cake, 12
 Sour Cream Coffee Cake, 4

Texas Sheet Cake, Classic, 80
Texas Tornado Cake, 92
toffee
 Oreo Icebox Dessert, 189

Ultimate Cookie Layer Cake, 198
Upside-Down Cake, Pineapple, 61

Vanilla Cake Roll, Christmas, 218
Vanilla Mug Cake, Moist, 156
vanilla wafers
 Banana Pudding Poke
  Cake, 147
Victoria Sponge Cake, 66
vinegar
 Lemon Crazy Cake, 54
vodka
 1970s Harvey Wallbanger Cake, 53

walnut(s)
 Church Cake, 88
 Cinnamon Cream Cheese Apple
  Cake, 115
white chocolate
 Cookies 'n' Cream Mug Cake, 159

yogurt
 Birthday Funfetti Layer
  Cake, 201
 Lime Bundt Cake, 21

Zucchini Cake with Browned Butter
 Frosting, 100

About the Author

After receiving her masters in culinary arts at Auguste Escoffier in Avignon, France, Addie stayed in France to learn from Christian Etienne at his three–Michelin star restaurant. Upon leaving France she spent the next several years working with restaurant groups. She worked in the kitchen for Daniel Boulud and moved coast to coast with Thomas Keller, building a career in management, restaurant openings, and brand development. She later joined Martha Stewart Living Omnimedia, where she worked with the editorial team as well as in marketing and sales. While living in New York, Addie completed her bachelor's degree in organizational behavior. Upon leaving New York, Addie joined gravitytank, an innovation consultancy in Chicago. As a culinary designer at gravitytank, Addie designed new food products for companies, large and small. She created edible prototypes for clients and research participants to taste and experience, some of which are in stores today. In 2015, she debuted on *The Food Network*, where she competed on *Cutthroat Kitchen*, and won! In 2017, she competed on the thirteenth season of *Food Network Star*.

Addie is the executive producer for RecipeLion. Addie oversees and creates culinary content for the multiple web platforms and communities, leads video strategy, and manages the production of in-print books. Addie is passionate about taking easy recipes and making them elegant, from fine dining to entertaining.

Addie and her husband live in Lake Forest, Illinois, with their baby boy and happy puppy, Paisley. Addie is actively involved with youth culinary programs in the Chicagoland area, serving on the board of a bakery and catering company that employs at-risk youth. She is a healthy food teacher for first-graders in a low-income school district and aside from eating and entertaining with friends and family, she loves encouraging kids to be creative in the kitchen.